REJOICE

A Biblical Study Of The Dance

by

Debbie Roberts

REVIVAL PRESS
Shippensburg, PA 17257

Cover Photography: Thomas Allison

Revival Press
Worship and Praise Division
of
Destiny Image Publishers
P.O. Box 351
Shippensburg, PA 17257

Fifth printing:	1989	Seventh printing: 1994
Sixth printing:	1992	

ISBN 0-938612-02-6

For Worldwide Distribution
Printed in the U.S.A.

Inside the U.S., call toll free to order:
1-800-722-6774

A DANCER

Shine! Shine! In the dark of night, white array!
Like the starlight high above, beyond this sphere,
A glowing halo was as they appeared.
For they stood in a circle, each in their place, perfect unity.
Fitly joined by His grace.
Always the Captain led them in step.
Motion and sound were one, as the beat was kept.

Expression, like unto the same without blemish,
Without sorrow, without defeat. . . and without blame.
Sparkles of gold fell from the hand,
Falling down to the earth,
Spreading out on the land and the masses gathered.
Searching the sky "from where did this gold come?"
Did they cry.
"Did it fall from the stars to this earth below?
Come let us arise and go higher that we may know."
The higher they arose, the thicker it did fall.
Covered by its showery brilliance were they all.
"Truly this must be from the Lord!", they sang.
It is blessing and riches that He brang.
And great joy broke loose as the crowd shouted praise.
None were left feeble, peaceful glow on their faces.
And the dance was continued, until the Lord spoke its end,
For they were called to His purpose, till He cometh again.

Lorrie Gray Mullins to Dance Company
August 1978

DEDICATION

This book is dedicated to my wonderful husband who encouraged me all the way through this book. From the very beginning of the word of the Lord, Gary stood in confidence with me that this was the way of the Lord for me. Sometimes when I was filled with confusion and doubt, he stood strong, knowing God would be faithful concerning His promise. Gary was patient and supportive of my time involved in study and learning. He still provides that extra little push I sometimes need to rise up in confidence and freely perform all that God has spoken concerning dance in the House of the Lord. For this, I am happy, grateful, and thankful. . .

I love you,
Debbie

A special thank you to my friend and fellow dancer Joni Miller from Shiloh Christian Fellowship in Oakland, California. Captain of the Expressive Worship Team, Joni's organization of personal notes on the "Function of a Dance Company" were extremely helpful in explaining the function of a company. I could not have written them in any better order myself. Thank you Joni!

ACKNOWLEDGEMENTS

TO MARLENE: My trusted friend who was a great strength and encourager concerning the "vision of the Lord." The hours of time you spent with me seeking God for truth will never be forgotten, and your support when others doubted meant everything to me. Thank you for believing and receiving by faith what God wanted to give.

TO JANET: My Pastor and friend who many times called me on the phone just to say, "we're with you, keep pressing in." Your faith in me was also responsible for keeping the vision of the dance alive and strong. Thank you for trusting God and hearing His direction for me. I love you. . .

TO SANDY: MY CO-CAPTAIN: and fellow dancer in the house of the Lord, a bearer of truth and righteousness. You believed all along from the beginning and that confidence helped. You are one of many who share the vision of the dance in the house of the Lord and I thank you for being there with me all along the way. Keep pressing in. . . God has more for you to do, Sandy, in this area.

TO SUSAN T.: MY CO-CAPTAIN: and fellow dancer. Thank you for taking the company while I was working on this book. You are a comfort to me, a strength to me, a labourer with me, and my friend. . .thank you for being with me, I praise God for you. . .

CONTENTS

PREFACE

Like many pastors and Christian leaders, I learned little about praise and worship in my denomination. The subject of dancing was forbidden and certainly unfit behavior for a Christian. Having a desire to be accepted by the brethren coupled with the fear of becoming unbalanced, only the Holy Spirit could have opened my heart to this Biblical truth.

In 1976, I was invited to be a guest speaker at Shiloh Christian Fellowship in Oakland, California. The service began in a traditional fashion. The song leader started the choir and congregation singing a familiar chorus. As our hearts were lifted up toward heaven in the form of praise comfortable to my convictions, a clap began to break out in a cadence, like the sound of a marching army. Soon our feet began to move to the same cadence. I opened my eyes and down the aisles came the dancers moving across the front near the altar. Their movements were descriptive. I watched, wept, and wondered, "Oh God, what is this?" They are acting out what the Holy Spirit is speaking in clear articulate steps. Each hand movement is interpreting to the audience the meaning of God's message. I was so delighted I called for my wife and daughter to join me the next morning. During the next three days, God confirmed and convicted us for our doubts and reservations.

Returning to our pastorate, we began to share, having a charismatic congregation, filled with Baptists, Nazarenes, and a sprinkling of Pentecostals. Our freshly found faith was delightful at first, then became distasteful. Then came Debbie Roberts, (now a close friend), to our fellowship and God opened her heart to research this beautiful subject. I owe a debt of gratitude to her for her faith and deep convictions which birthed our congregation and this timely book. As her pastor, I am thankful she stood in the gap to open this truth to our body. It was her determination in the midst of doubt and disbelief that has brought us into this beautiful form of worship. It is my prayer that God will use this book to instruct many to "Rejoice!"

Pastor Tony Alward
Christian Center Chapel
Claremont, California

INTRODUCTION

The Dance. A simple concept, yet majestic in interpretation. What is this new activity in the church? Is it really new? Is this being birthed by the Holy Spirit or has the church become more liberal? These are a few of the questions many people ask when they hear the term dance connected with the church. Some may use more moderate terms like choreography or choir movement or drama. I am talking about real dance. Free movement whether ballet, modern, or Hebrew. Any type that flows with the message of the Word of the Lord through song.

It is my estimation that the dance, as a mode of worship, will grow with magnitude and swiftness that will astound many conservative church members. There is a place for this expression in it's simple most beautiful form in a conservative service, just as there is room for a modern musical presentation as a tool for evangelism. We will see the dance take many forms in the next few years.

Early man knew no difference between dance that was natural and dance that was spiritual. Dance was a part of his everyday life; a part of his worship, a part of his warfare. As the early religious leaders brought weighty rules and regulations, the joy of the Holy Spirit fled and separation was caused between religion and existence. Therefore dance was termed totally natural and had no part in religious ceremony.

I thank God that in His infinite grace and mercy He is restoring this mode of expression to His Church. What wonderful days we live in! Days of restoration. Days of enjoying God's presence. Days of seeing skill and artistry restored to His Church. In years past when the "charismatic" movement was at its peak, the music in the church could slide by on the anointing. I don't mean to belittle the anointing. It is the anointing that will release, deliver and heal. Without Jesus' anointing on our music and our dance, we minister in vain. I would like to bring to attention skill and artistry plus anointing. Let's move into perfection. Let's see the arts restored to the church. Let's use these tools for Jesus and His Glory. All the earth will behold His Glory.

Now that you know my personal feelings, how do I go about describing one of the most wonderful experiences of my life? Being part of this vision has been thrilling, exciting, rewarding and at times trying. The probitive finger of God's hand continues to press my spirit to reach further than my natural eye can see. Sometimes haunting questions linger in the back of my mind: "Could this really be what you desire Lord? Am I progressing correctly?" How wonderful if this whole experience is true! It's almost too much fun. But you know, it is true. The vision is correct. God is blessing it and it is full of joy. God has met my searchings time and time again with warmth of assurance, love, and anointing. This is why I was created. This is my purpose in life - to be a worshipper of the MOST HIGH GOD!

Sometimes I don't understand all this vision entails, yet I still believe. I am confident that as we continue to walk in Jesus' light, this progressive revelation will unfold.

WHAT IS DANCE?

According to the American College Dictionary, the word dance means:

1)   move the feet or rest of the body rhythmically, especially to music.
2)   to skip, leap, etc. as from excitement or emotion, move nimbly or quickly.
3)   to bob up and down.
4)   to perform or take part in a dance.

Dance will be the exact expression of the person doing the movement. To the unregenerated soul, dance will be expression of a void performance. To the Spirit of a born-again Christian, dance will be the expression of that Spirit. The dance will communicate Spirit to Spirit with those interpreting praise unto God.

Dance can be complex or simple. Dance combines thoughts of the heart and motor coordination to bring forth a structure of movement. As this structure takes form, it is called patterned movement or dance. Whether marching, walking, or swaying, this is structured movement in time and space called dance. God is always a God of pattern. There was a pattern for the tabernacle, a pattern for Solomon's Temple, and a plan of salvation for men to follow. Dance has pattern and order just as music does. When dance takes on a visible structure and a sequence of movement, it can be received and understood. Onlookers will be able to discern by the message the visible

expression. Dance. . . dance is expression that is to bring a
clear message.

Let's examine the beginning of dance, where it came
from, and how it can be used today. We will go back to the
book of *Genesis* for our first example. We know that *Genesis*
is the seed bed for every major truth or doctrine found in the
Bible. Since God created music and dance, reference to both is
found in *Genesis.*

> *"And his brother's name was Jubal: he was the father of*
> *all such as handle the harp and organ."*
>
> *Genesis 4:21*

This is one of three beginning professions on the earth.
Jubal's name in the original Hebrew means: 1) to flow as a
stream; 2) especially with pomp, and 3) to bring forth, to
lead. [1] His brothers listed with him are "Tubalcain," an instructor of every artificer in brass and iron, and "Jabal,"
the father of such that dwell in tents, and of such as have
cattle. So we see three beginning professions; music, smith
and shepherd.

Next we see in *Genesis 2:11* the land of Havilah.

> *"The name of the first is Pison: that is it which compas-*
> *seth the whole land of Havilah, where there is gold. . ."*

Havilah in Hebrew means: 1) circular; 2) from the prim
root word to twist, or whirl in a circular or spiral manner,
and 3) to dance, writhe in pain.[2] The next mention in *Gene-*
sis is in *Chapter 5:12:*

> *"And Cainan lived seventy years and begat Mahalalee..."*

The root meaning of Mahalalee in Hebrew is 1) praise of
God; 2) fame, praise; 3) to be clear of sound; 4) to shine

---

1 Strong's Concordance 2986
2 Strong's Concordance 2341, 2342

forth and 5) make a show, to boast, to celebrate, to be clamorously foolish. [3]

There is no doubt that music and dance were created by God. To dance is the physical or outward expression of the inward relationship or experience with the Lord. Patterned movement is the vehicle in which that inner experience can become an outward expression. To dance is to use technique, form, and expression to communicate to others that experience with the Lord. The Lord says we are to show forth the praises of our God.

"That I may show forth all thy praise in the gates of the daughter of Zion: I will rejoice in thy salvation."
Psalms 9:14

"Oh Lord, open thou my lips; and my mouth will show forth thy praise."
Psalms 51:15

"So we thy people and sheep of thy pasture will give thee thanks forever: we will show forth thy praise to all generations."
Psalms 79:13

"This people have I formed for myself; they shall show forth my praise."
Isaiah 43:21

". . . and they shall shew forth the praises of the Lord."
Isaiah 60:6

Dance is one of the ways we can show forth the praises of our God. In scripture, we are commanded by God to dance before Him.

---

3 Strong's Concordance 410, 4110, 4111

"Let them praise his name in the dance: let them sing praises unto him with the timbrel and harp."
Psalms 149:3, Psalms 150:4

"They have seen thy goings, O God; even the goings of my God, my King, in the Sanctuary. The singers went before, the players on instruments followed after; among them were the damsels playing with timbrels."
Psalms 68:24-25

There are so many scriptures that exhort us, the church, to make an open declaration of praise and worship to our King. We are to perform our vows in the sanctuary, in the midst of our brethren.

"My praise shall be of thee in the great congregation. I will pay my vows before them that fear him."
Psalms 22:25

"I will pay my vows unto the Lord now in the presence of all his people, in the courts of the Lord's house, in the midst of thee, O Jerusalem. Praise ye the Lord."
Psalms 116:18-19

How will the world view the church of our Lord Jesus when they recognize people rejoicing in their God?

When the word "dance" is spoken, your mind paints for you a picture. What do you see? You will see dance fit for God's Kingdom or dance fit for the kingdom of darkness. Maybe the picture your mind paints reveals a partial truth, i.e. you see dance, yet certainly not in the church; or the picture is beautiful and speaks to you, saying, "Why can't this be done in the sanctuary?"

Throughout the generations, the meaning of dance has changed according to the age that produced it. For example, if your heart and mind were set on the flapper era of the "twenties," your mind would paint a picture of the Charleston. If the same were true of the "fifties," you would paint a picture of the Twist. We can understand the way our mind works by this example. Similarly, if you come from a very traditional church background, dance expression as an act of praise and worship will be something you must examine. Christ has given us His mind for the purpose of discernment:

> *"For who hath known the mind of the Lord, that he may instruct him? But we have the mind of Christ."*
> *I Corinthians 2:16*

> *"Let this mind be in you, which was also in Jesus Christ."*
> *Philippians 2:5*

Our mind is renewed daily through the power of God's Word. Our mind does not need to be rooted in century-old ritual and liturgy. With the restoration of David's Tabernacle, God is allowing many art forms to be restored to His Church. A total work of restoration began it's working in us when we accepted Jesus. Pretty soon the old songs cease to be sung and our hearts bring forth out of our mouth a new song - a song unto our God; a song of praise. So also can our mind bring forth a new picture of dance. A dance of joy in Jesus, a dance of hope and trust, a dance of victory with clapping, a dance of love flowing. Ask the Lord Jesus to paint for you a new picture of the dance. I am confident He will.

Every local church can have some expression of movement. Should music and dance merge the effect would be unity of "praise unto God." The picture becomes clear and precise. St. Augustine in the year 390 expressed hope that the musicians, choir, and dancers could work in unity. Many Greek dancers continue to sing as they dance. The steps match the rhythm of the words or phrases and not the musical structure. This is what our reference talks about in the Bible of dancing chorus.

Any art form begins with a purpose and grows through experience and technique. A church could start using movement as a means of expression by beginning with a simple choir procession. What a nice change to have the choir enter in from down the aisle instead of filing in from the side of the church. Our bodies can be the very instrument or vessel and the simplest movement is the mode of communication. Movement will always enhance, enlarge and add impact to what is being sung or played. Also consider using banners, flags, etc.

Let's look at simple arm or hand expressions to a chorus. Once again a whole choir could be taught to use their hands on selected choruses. Eventually you'll find the whole congregation will want to participate. When this happens a new dimension of praise and worship will be released in your congregation. People will become less aware of themselves and concentrate more on the Lord. A new sense of unity will prevail. God will visit the people who praise Him openly.

What is the purpose of dance, you may ask? Why use it at all and what does it accomplish? First of all, we are commanded by God to praise Him in the dance. This command stands alone. But God knew how man operated. The Lord certainly doesn't NEED a bunch of people worshipping Him in the dance. He enjoys it. He accepts it. He joins with us (Zephaniah 3:17); however in His infinite wisdom He knew what expression through movement would do for US! As we release ourselves to praise Him with voice, with instruments, or bodies, we are lifted into His presence. This transforms our thinking and our lives.

From glory to glory He is changing me. . .

Doctors now use and recommend dance therapy for treatment. These therapists examine the patients' speech, eye contact, gestures and walk. After observing these movements, steps are choreographed to bring about needed changes. For example, one who is depressed, lethargic and withdrawn would need fast, stimulating steps. Over the months the person's personality was corrected. This new practice is taking place all over the country in psychiatric wards, day centers and rehabilitation centers. Dance therapy was started in the early 1940's. Doctors do not deny its healing "miracles" for their patients.

Even in the natural sense, doctors know that through movement one can express what cannot be spoken. Dance can bring the emotional release; the response so desired. The body and mind are intertwined and what affects one usually surfaces in the other. Our bodies are a reflection of what is happening on the inside. Dance has effects on the body which operate like physical exercise. It causes the blood to circulate, activates thinking, quickens the heartbeat; one feels alive and vibrant. Oh how the Lord knew this and wants this for His Church! Not a sluggish, sleeping Church, but one alive and flowing. Praise through song and movement will accomplish all this and more!

II

HISTORY OF THE SOCIAL DANCE

Dance has always been a by-product of society. It has a close relationship to social and economic changes. Anxieties, fears, joys, sorrows and many other humanly characterisitics affect its social dance. Upheaval in dress and fashion have a strong bearing on dance. Nearly every dance revealed has been ushered in with hysteria and daring. Along with each wave came hair styles, fashion changes, and make-up to support each new age. They became an acceptable mode of expression. What we saw twenty years ago has now become old-fashioned and certainly not shocking at all. This is an accepted general principle and if we apply it specifically to dance, it is frightening.

Social dance sprang from the 1600-1700 early court dances or balls. All the courts of Europe while trying to outdo each other, conjuring up the most elaborate balls. Dress accompanied the trend, causing some ladies to hurt their backs under the strain of such a load of clothing and jewelry. Great bouffant wigs accompanied the grandeur as the crowning touch.

Dance masters were hired to dignify the peasant dances. These masters taught music, dance, exquisite dress and polished manners as well.

From the 1700 ballrooms we travel on to the very beginning of the frontier tavern. The early settlers of America thought it very proper to send children "home" to England to learn the latest social skills. There always seemed a division between those settlers who wanted to rid themselves of all past ties and those who still hung onto their former ways and manners. Many of these New England Puritan settlers came to America with strong Calvinistic ideals. To them, dance, drama and music had no place among any of their beliefs.

We find a split in America's early beginning - one that travels three ways. To some, the latest court dances of Europe became part of their new American culture. To others, the tavern of the wild west became American dance. And to still others within the church, music and dance had no place at all.

It is so strong how new ideas become twisted. Music was being suppressed yet it was never supposed to be. Our history books tell us that these new Americans arrived with over 300 volumes of music and many instruments.

The middle 1800's show the social dance of the West; the can can and square dance emerge. This honky-tonk, blazing the trail effect became associated with alcohol and dance hall girls. With this "evil effect," social dance began to take a nose dive. It never recovered its respectable esteem. Night clubs are the offspring of this era.

Around 1739, the blacks began using syncopation. They were forbidden to use drums so they transferred the rhythm to their feet.

It is no wonder the church frowned on anything that had to do with rhythm or dance. There is no question that the Protestant Reformation supressed the arts. Historians are now re-examining personal records to see if there was a thread of restorational dance allowed in any church.

During this time balls, social dances, and get-togethers became frequent. Each town seemed to have its own barn dance. The square dance and other social dances became very popular now. During the late 1800's, America began to produce her own traveling dance teachers. One unique example is the beginning of the square dance term "honor your partner." This mannerism came directly from the court dances of the 1600. Another item still used is the curtsey. These are both examples of court manners mixed with early American custom.

By the 1900's the folk aspect of dance was dying out. From this date on we begin to reap wilder social dances. The wars of the early 1900's brought great military balls. These were a highlight and along the same line as the early court dances.

Let's look at a few of the social dances of America and see if we can understand how dance travels a definite pattern.

A.   Fox Trot (1900 -) This was a fast trotting step to a new beat, "rag time." It became a very popular dance and the rag time sound challenged many compositions with a new sound.

B.   Charleston (1920 -) This music was a combination of fast dixieland and jazz. This dance brought along with it the short haircut, the shorter dress and the whole "Flapper" look. These dances were strenuous and had many tricky feet movements. It attracted all ages.

C.   Big Band Era (1930 - 40) The Fox Trot had been perfected, the waltz livened up and the popular dances became the swing and the jitterbug. The hearts of the American people were captured. Dance studios sprang up. Large public ballrooms were established and social dance was now a part of the physical education department of every school in America.

D.   Latin (1950 - 60) Toward the end of the 1950's the Latin craze hit our country. Trips to Mexico, Spanish food, the "bossa nova." tango, mambo, calypso, and cha cha all became popular standards within social dances.

E.   Rock and Roll - In the mid 60's the military draft became the force behind our next transition in the social dance. This war caused the big bands to reduce their size to the smaller "combo." Tiny dance floors of clubs replaced the large ballroom. Rhythm and blues had a strong growth during this time. Coffee houses, discotheques and clubs began to spring up because of the demand for social dancing. The rock and roll craze began here and was labeled an hysterical fad. There was a general new feeling about dance. That active, driving beat did away with courtesy and began to gnaw at morals.

F.   Disco (1970-80) The last trend that is still on the

increase is the independent spirit manifested in the social dances of the Disco. Rock and roll had a partner, but Disco started with one, doing away with the partner and highlighting a lone dancer doing his or her thing. Frizzed hair, exotic clothes, strobe lights and unencumbered pattern of movement, all have a bearing on the changing social values. This is a reflection of our society and the influence of self-gratifcation. Punk began in England a few years ago and most Americans labeled it bizarre. Now in this year of 80-81, we are seeing it commonly. Its follow-up callenge, beginning to overtake punk in England is "Blitz." This behavior and social value is even farther out than Punk. It is "anything goes" behavior and dress. Music at ear-splitting levels, dance that mingles mime and robot movements, costumes that are to "create your own look." Normal people or show people are not admitted to these clubs. It is only for the "far out." It is an escape route designed to shock and entertain.

BALLET

What is ballet? Many have misconception of this term and I suppose it's because of what they have seen with their eyes. The root word for ballet is French and Italian. It was an elaborate party with music, poetry and dance. Later, this type of celebration was entitled a ballet. There could be any type of dance done here, along with mime, songs or drama. Country folk dances were also very popular at one's backyard "ballet." This was a social affair of banquets and fireworks that friends and family could attend. These gatherings sometimes lasted two to three days.

As time progressed, the social dances became a little more difficult. The dancers needed to keep a slightly turned out foot and leg to hold better balance. Here is where the first technique was formed. It's the same principle as all folk dance, being done with the knees slightly bent. Ballet at this point began to become nothing more than the Minuet or other social country dance developed and polished.

A pattern of steps were written down around the 1600's and became the foundation for all ballet exercises today. The same steps are used as technique training tools all over the world. Ballet has become a language without words. Each step is directed, making a pattern of well ordered dance steps. This ballet dance is a dance that places emphasis on carriage and manners. A book entitled The English Dancing Master, circa 1650, by John Playford reveals the strict etiquette and technique required of a dance.

King Louis XIV of France learned dance at a young age. He became an accomplished dancer and appeared in many court ballets. Because of his court duties he had to stop the pursuit of dance. By the time he was 30 he was so overweight he couldn't dance at all. This led to hiring "professional dancers." Here is the first thrust toward professional dance and the first dance school. The construction of a large ballroom moved the dance to become a social affair for the elite. King Louis lived to be 77 years old. He was never sick and attributed this fact to his exercise in the dance.

In 1661, King Louis set up the first Academy for Dance, because he felt dance should be developed as an art. Ballet was moving now out of the amateur range and into a position of skill.

> *"The art of dance has ever been acknowledged to be one of the most suitable and necessary arts for physical development and for affording the primary and most natural preparation for all bodily exercise, and among others, those including the use of weapons and consequently it is one of the most valuable and most useful arts for nobles and others who have the honor to enter our presence, (the King, not only in time of war in our armies, but even in time of peace in our ballets.)"*
> *Louis XIV*

Ballet teachers in beginning were muse and poet, royal princes, dancers, choreographers and composers. Therefore, ballet was supplied by the finest music; frequently the violin played by the dancing Master himself. King Louis XIV's composer was a man named Lully, an accomplished dancer as well. Eventually, each court in the land had its own troop of dancers, singers, musicians and acrobats. Pierre Beauchamp became the first instructor of this school of dance. He was called the Court Dancing Master. He established the five positions of the feet.

The dance grew with great popularity in the early 1700's. From the simple plays came great, lavish spectacles. The King and courtiers were the principle performers. Noblemen were expert at dancing and mime and took early training from the court teachers. Music existed to serve the steps of the dancer. Rhythm and harmony left music at this time. The music was very ordered and unadventurous. It was uncomplicated and supplied by "house" composers.

An example of the theatre spectacular shows put on in Italy during the early 1700 was a massive theatre performance that left the whole state near bankruptcy. An entire arena was flooded to the depth of three feet for the finale of the Battle of the Sea Monsters. Then, about one hundred people descended from the ceiling on a cloud. Another example was a show with the use of eighteen horses, two elephants, an ox and a cast of five hundred dancers.

In 1707-1756, a lady named Marie Salle, a French choreographer and very popular dancer, began to use Greek costuming while she danced. In London, during 1710-1770, Marie Camargo shortened her ballet skirt to mid-calf.

There is a thread through dance of spiritual hunger. Most referred to Greek mythology to try to capture this void as they danced. Later in the ballet there was a Biblical awakening in dance and themes, but it was viewed as a spiritual experience as simple as Greek mythology with no truth or heart devotion.

The area of court dances became very popular in the late 1700's. A man named Domenico listed 12 basic steps with 21 different dances. His pupil, William the Jew from Pesaro, became a sought after dance master. Another court dancer and teacher was named Cesare Negri, nicknamed "the Trombone." He was a very exclusive teacher and traveled extensively.

By this time, dance had become part of every level of society. Most all European countries had dance schools and theatres. Opera and ballet were most popular. During the 1790's, dancers began to use the face mask. Dance was done very stiffly with complete strictness. Quite a different story than King David's dance of the Bible. This period was called "The Age of Enlightenment." During this time France became the leader of ethics, dress, literature and dance. John Weaver was the first to write down the historical perspective of dance steps to music. Around the 1700's, he developed a notation system that brought order to teaching dance. He also saw the use of drama used with ballet and encouraged his students to tell stories with movement. Music and costumes became something important. The first ballet was based on these principles.

The face mask was still used until a Frenchman, Noverr, battled his way through to bring about new freedom. He rid the dance of the mask and allowed flowing arm movements. This spread throughout Europe and reached schools in Russia established under Catherine the Great.

Ballet master Charles Le Picq, trained serfs; many of which were sold to the Imperial theatres in Moscow for dance. The last recorded sale was in 1806. These early ballet dances were brimming with mythology. Cupids, nymphs and terpsichore led the story line of most ballets. In 1793, Italian choreographer Salvatore Vigano and his wife introduced drapes and flesh colored tights. They appeared nude when they danced and this led the way to rid dance of heavy Brocade panties and petticoats. Costumes became flowing chiffon.

At the close of the 1700's, the French revolution put to death much dance, especially the ballet. It became unpopular because it was labeled for courts and noblemen. The people wanted social folk dance to take its place. In 1830, some 15 years after Napoleon came into office, the revival of ballet captured France. The first use of toe shoes or point shoes became known here. Marie Taglioni was the first to publically dance on her toes.

Toward the end of the 1800's around 1875, a new breakthrough came to pass with the music of Tchaikovsky. His writing brought forth a unity between choreography and music. His most memorable ballet was Swan Lake. Writers said this man lived the pace of the dancer and understood deep feelings of movement. He was high strung, self-critical, and very complex.

America and England were the only countries at this time which had no training program subsidized by the state. Consequently, American students were at the mercy of ill-prepared teachers. The first American home-grown ballet star was Mary Ann Lee. Another was Agusta Maywood, who was only 15 at her Paris debut. Theatre ballet required less and began to be performed by inexperienced chorus girls from New York Music halls. The classical ballet in London and its meager beginning in America fell to nothing. One such example of this was the "skirt dance" developed by Lottie Collins. This dance of 1879 involved simple steps done in large flowing skirts. As some ladies became bolder, they added free flowing movement, only to end up on the floor after being caught in their skirts. This dance initiated the famous Can Can. As one may suspect, the dignified classical ballet became a circus act. Acrobatics were added along with overdone jewelry and ballet fell into disrepute. It took on the title of "naughty nineties" dancing. Self-respecting gentlemen would not come near this act and consequently all male roles were played by ladies dressed as gentlemen.

The only respectable ballet schools remaining at this time were the Soviet Russia schools. The Imperial government payed for all the schools and theatres. During the late 1800's, Russia began to import competent ballet masters from Europe. Because of the decline of dance in Europe, this was a welcome challenge for them and they departed gladly. Russia now had excellent teachers and with the help of the state, professional ballet flourished.

The Russian revolution in 1917 held three popular opinions for the people:

> A.   Destroy by extreme everything pertaining to the old Imperial way of life. The fine arts should be preserved for the sake of the people. State-owned

ballet schools remained open.

B. The general public was not educated in the arts because it was previously available to a tiny minority of people. Now concerts and ballets were sent to every major republic to enlighten the people.

C. They found that ballets would be politically appropriate to the revolution and theatrically accepted by the public masses. At first, the teachers discarded classical rules and technique, but this bred dancers of no value.

Because of the large revolution taking place in Soviet Russia, the country began to detach itself from the mainstream of what was taking place around the world in the arts. She did not evolve but withdrew. As a result she is considered to be about five years behind in modern arts. Her technique and ability, however, are considered the best in the world. Because of this withdrawal, many dancers and choreographers left that country and went to Monte Carlo. Here creativity was allowed to flow unhindered of the Revolution.

One of the most noted names in Russian Ballet is Galena Vlanova. She was born in 1910, the daughter of two Imperial dancers of Maryinsky Theatre. She resisted ballet school, which consisted of rooming in and hardly any play time, but soon adapted and proved to be one of the country's greatest dancers. Soviets have an excellent generation-to-generation training school system.

I might add here that all ballet training is universal. All steps are known as technique styles and the only difference is in concept. An example is:

English Schools

Likes the effect of effortless
Teaches to float freely
Always a plot and theme

American Schools

Speed and agility
No main story
Theme needed, will not relate
Abstract

Soviet Schools   Classical Ballet

High leaps and much strength   *Simply those old ballets pro-*
Always a story line and plot - *duced in Russia*
Relate to people
Acrobatic style with partner

The Ballet Russe was the first traveling company of
artists who didn't really have a home base. Because of the in-
flux of artists to Monte Carlo due to the revolution, these
people banded together to perform. This was the birth of the
road companies we see today. These dancers were powerful
personalities who gave their all. They blazed a trail through
London, Paris, Great Britain and America. They brought vision
and hope to the American Ballet, and this theatre group became responsible for our American Ballet Theatre.

American men thought ballet was great, but felt that
only foreign men could dance. . .certainly not American men!
During this time, American choreographers began to create
ballets with American themes such as Rodeo, Billy the Kid,
Fancy Free, and others. American men began to take note.
Russian masters and choreographers arrived and the American
technique improved.

Our twentieth century first classical danseur (male
dancer) was Erik Bruhn. He came from the oldest ballet
school, still open today, in Copenhagen. He had great influence
on ballet and after the wars led London to become the ballet
capital of the world.

Ballet dancers were looked upon as extremely fit
athletically. The ballerina, who held the spotlight for centuries,
now begins to fade and male strength is recaptured.

American ballet had become idle - until Rudolf Nureyev.
He especially caused men to take a second look at ballet.
This stirring brought to an end nearly one hundred years of
dance without a male image.

Another popular male influence is Mikail Baryshnikov.
He is a free-flowing stylist with strong technique from the
Leningrad school. His influence caused over 20 million people

to see the ballet.

In summary, I would describe this style of dancing as an inner response portrayed by structure, form and a secure balance demonstrated in beautiful arm and head movements. Ballet is an art developed by training, demanding strict discipline and bringing the body under subjection of the dancer. It is a beautiful expression in its God-ordained form.

THE FOLK DANCE

Folk dance is the traditional dance of a people. No longer is this restricted to national boundaries or peasant lifestyles. This dance is for the dancer first, the spectator second and thirdly, communication. Many took part - young, old, men, children and women. The folk dance is not taught very much these days. In days of old most folk dance was led by the men. Countries today cannot produce even one folk dance of their land.

We are beginning however to see a new surge of interest in this area as people are restoring it as a recreational activity. For the Christian there is a special joy in learning the Israeli dances. Since Israel lost her identity for so many years, her dances reveal both eastern and western influences.

From the beginning, Jewish dance has been a part of the religious experience. Even today the dance is a part of every child's education. To the Jews, dance was always a prayer accompanied by music, singing or beating of the drums. There is frequent reference to the dance in the Old and New Testament. Processionals, ritual dances, dances of religious ecstasy, dances of vintage, harvest, joy, praise, thanksgiving and warfare are just a few of the dances done by these people. The Hebrew people are called dancing masters. These masters were leaders in teaching dance during the middle ages. Their responsibilities were to organize, teach and lead in the dance.

There are three main categories to the Jewish Dance. The first is the Hassidic. This is a style inspired by the early life of the prophets. It was a dance of spontaneous ecstasy, showing inner exultation. A means of religious expression, this dance leaped from the hearts of devout believers. It would release the prophetic flow and bring the anointing of the Holy Spirit. It was used by the prophets and was probably taught with music at the school of the prophets.

> *"And David danced before the Lord with all his might; and David was girded with a linen ephod."*
>
> II Samuel 6:14

> *"And he stripped off his clothes also, and prophesied before Samuel in like manner, and layed down naked all that day and all that night. Wherefore they say, is Saul also among the prophets?"*
>
> I Samuel 19:24

> *"After that thou shalt come to the hill of God, where is the garrison of the Philistines: and it shall come to pass, when thou art come thither to the city, that thou shall meet a company of prophets coming down from the high place with a psaltery, and a tabret (or tambourine) and a pipe, and a harp, before them; and they shall prophesy: And the Spirit of the Lord will come upon thee, and thou shalt prophesy with them, and shalt be turned into another man."*
>
> I Samuel 10:5-6

The Hassadic dance surfaced during the 18th century in Poland. As devout Jewish men sought God they began to dance. They did not sing words while they danced because they felt words could not express what the heart felt so deeply. Movement and improvision could bring the release.

The second main Hebrew dance is called the Yeminite. This dance was totally different from the Hassidic. It was a very graceful dance with flowing movements and a beautiful pattern. This dance became a way of life and a flowing prayer movement. Of the Hebrew dances, the Yeminite was the most fluid. This beautiful style of dance was "rebirthed" from S.W.

Arabia or Aden in 1910 & 1949. It was the Yeminite Jew who stayed closest to his roots. His traditions and ceremonies have almost remained the same since Bible days. They have retained the cultural patterns of the ancient Hebrews. These dances are slower in rhythm with gentle flowing arm and hand movements. Sometimes they would gradually accelerate to drums, hand clapping and singing. Beautifully embroidered handwork on garments are part of this group's culture. The dance is marked by a penchant for beauty, song and poetry.

The third dance of Israel is called the Debka. These dances consisted of intricate, difficult footwork. A drumming rhythm of Arab origin caused the dancers to dance with strength. These people came back to Israel from Syria and Lebanon. The warlike effect received from this style caused many to receive strength and rise up to dance in power and might.

The Hora is probably the most well-known Hebrew dance. It is the national dance of Israel. Done to the accompaniment of hand clapping, the music frequently speeds up. A mixed orchestra is used by the Hebrews.

The rise and revival of Israeli dance started in 1944 with the first annual dance festival. It was used to draw people from different countries back to a national common heritage. As David long ago, so has Israel discovered today the impact of dance in growth, establishment and unity.

"In the beginnings, the dancer inevitably sings as he dances. . .When, however, his movements become too strenuous and demand too much breath for him to continue his song the bystanders take up the singing for him. In time the melodic line of the voice is transferred to an instrument and since it can play higher and lower than he could possibly sing, it serves even to increase his range of expression. Similarly, the rhythmic beating of his feet on the ground is accentuated and intensified past what he could do himself, by the clapping of hands, the shaking of rattles, and the beating of drums, if it is really dance music it still remains the rhythmic pulse of

his body and the melodic line of his voice. It is indeed potentially the dancer's own song."

Excerpt from <u>The Dance</u>, by John Martin
Tudor Publishing Company

Folk dance began to decline as a pastime of the people. Hungary and probably elsewhere, folk dance was used by the national army as means of recruiting. They would march into a town and perform folk dances in the city square. Local youths would join in and the best dancers were given priority by officers for special positions because of their alertness and activeness. Today the Red Army choir and dance troupe is a permanent theatrical group.

The Industrial revolution took swift hold of these light-footed young men. It pulled them out of the fields and into the factories. Since there is no traditional dance of the factory learned and handed down from generation to generation, celebrations and festivals began to see fewer and fewer dances. In order to lift heavy burdens and add flavor to a routine life, men and women began to look to the Saturday night social affair. Dance was taken out of the country and away from the people, causing a void. This void was replaced with a Saturday night dance. Men began to take part less and less. An English critic from 1911 said, "I'd rather be caught in the act of stealing than dancing." Roles were totally reversed now. Men used to dance to win girls, but now, the ladies all danced to win the men. The strength and ability were now given to the women. Another hindrance that forced the male influence away from dance was the birth of the Waltz. Here the woman became "a partner" in the man's arms. He became encumbered and was no longer free to dance. Another dance called the Allemande required the man to hold his partner's hand continually.

Men became so removed from dance that in the early 1900's the women of the ballet had to do the man's part as well. To put a woman in a man's costume became so undignified all ballet when downhill briefly. The upper class began establishing the waltz. It was danced by peasants first and later sought out by nobility. This seems to be a principle of dance.

It is birthed in the "common people" and then socially adopted. When society becomes bored, they simply look to the commoners and gather up a new dance. The waltz was first greeted with horror and suspicion. Many respectable families would not permit their daughters to dance so close to a young man. It was termed the "voluptuous intertwining of the limbs, the close compressure of the bodies." But by 1837 the courts began using it and approval was given.

In 1840, the polka emerged from Czechoslovakia. This folk dance of the country spread to the social dance halls quickly. It was much more popular than our American Charleston or Twist. This dance was done lightly on the balls of the feet. The pivot step is also a common folk step along with the pas-de-basque or the "setting step."

In America around the same time, an American black man by the name of "Juba" broke forth in a new style: jazz. Jazz is a genuine folk culture of North America. North American folk art should logically come from Indian or European ancestry, but it didn't. Jazz is a combination of South American and African music and dance. Men instead of women excelled in jazz. The American ballet exhibits its influence because our twentieth century culture grew up with it. Russia hasn't and does not accept jazz as an art form. It is to be twenty years before Soviet and Western dance meet each other.

The 1900's began as the age of discarding everything. Out went the corsets, bloomers, petticoats, toe shoes and Victorian morality. Now comes free love, free votes, free transportation, free. . .you get the picture. Contemporary society flowed with the dance of its people. The Modern Dance was born. In 1907, a man named Rudolf Van Laban pioneered modern or contemporary dance. His interest was spiritual purpose of dance. He taught eurythmics, expressive body movement based on musical pattern. This was a departure from folk history and dance became a product of intellect instead of the heart. His followers included the Wiesenthal Sisters of 1907, Ruth St. Denis and Isadora Duncan. Another pupil of this study was Mary Wigman in 1928. She developed the "movement choir." Martha Graham, the "mother of modern dance" appears around this time.

Intellectual dance used unnatural rhythmic patterns to reveal the pulse of our living. This type of dance had no technique or universal notation system. Modern dance relates to ground movement whereas Folk dance uplifts. Modern dance prospered in America where ballet was considered too rigid and disciplined.

Time is ripe for a new mode of dance. Everyone was hungry for something special. Isadora Duncan arrives upon the scene.

Isadora Duncan was born in 1878 in California, one of four children. Her father deserted their family so her mother taught music to support them. From the time Isadora was small, she wanted to dance in her own way. With the encouragement of her mother, the whole family moved to New York and eventually Europe in pursuit of Isadora's dance desires. As Isadora grew older, she became more aware of her unique abilities and decided that only Hellenic Greece held the key that would launch her career. The whole Duncan family moved to Greece in 1903. At the age of 25, Isadora lived atop a hill near Athens. She had to be near the temple for Greek gods and she needed her own amphitheatre. She wanted to honor her Greek community so she planned to build a commune. Her desire was to live as old Greece did. She built a house and had plans for a small temple, theatre, library and dorms, but they were never realized.

As we examine the Greek culture, glorification of body and soul predominates. Idol worship and prostitution in the temples were prevalent. Isadora's elaborate plans and desires were not appreciated by the Greek community in which she lived. They did not accept this eccentric American trying to pull them back in time. For this reason and love of money Isadora moved to Paris. She traveled throughout Europe displaying her new dance style. People were caught by its desirous free-flowing movements. Isadora's goal in the past was to dance for her gods but the need for money was necessary to her lifestyle. Her life was torn by a double standard.

Isadora was invited to open a school in Russia to teach

this new style of dance. They wanted to see how modern dance was done. "Free dance" is what they called it. Its purpose in Russia was to compliment and help support the new young revolution of the state in 1920. However, the school fell through. The people could not accept movement without pattern, dances without a theme and the dresses of Greek gods. The only things the Russians gleaned from Isadora were her free flowing arm and head movements. The Russian people were idealistic people and any dance shown in the abstract was not accepted.

Isadora despised structured ballet and called herself a poet in motion. She was the first to bring dance and spiritualism together. She tried to return dance to its original purpose of worship but it was worship of idols and not our Lord Jesus.

She was not labeled a theatre artists for she enjoyed dancing in churches, gardens, at parties and at temples. She was termed by the theatre world as an amateur, yet there was great demand for her performances.

Isadora sought divine expression of the human spirit, and if she followed her instinct, she believed that she could become nature itself. She would become the sea, the wind, clouds, the sky. She worshipped the creature more than the creator.

"Wherefore God also gave them up to uncleanness through the lusts of their own hearts, to dishonor their own bodies between themselves: who changed the truth of God into a lie, and worshipped and served the creature more than the Creator, who is blessed for ever. Amen."

Romans 1:24-25

Isadora eventually had two children out of wedlock and both were killed as the car they were riding in slipped into a river. Isadora herself was killed when her long neck scarf became trapped in the wheel of a car driven by a young man she had recognized as a "messenger of the gods." Because she appeared during a time of strict discipline in dance, she was called by her contemporaries "the prophet of dance."

By her own admission, dance production was easy for her. She would receive and relate through the spirits. She would hear a melody from another world and through prayer and meditation, create a dance. She communicated her message in terms of movement. She could not bear the thought of using her instrument, her body, in such a constricted way as the ballet. Her dance was one of life and expression. Whatever impressions she received she danced. She strongly worshipped Greek gods and knew her "call" was to dance. Others who watched her became enlightened by her fluid power. She danced in thin silky drapes as the Greeks, usually blue. She danced with total abandon, and was viewed by many as floating in sunshine, her feet hardly touching the floor.

Her life was one of tragedy and moral corruption. Worship of idols leaves a person void of understanding and a victim of confusion. How sad to see one so dedicated yet so lost.

As we see disco with its Greek drape look I am reminded of a scripture in Zechariah which says:

> *"When I have bent Judah for me, filled the bow with Ephraim, and raised up thy sons, O Zion, against thy sons, O Greece, and made thee as the sword of a mighty man."*
>
> *Zechariah 9:13*

During the 1920's, it was the Charleston that released the male partner from the grasp of his lady. The Charleston affected every class. It had the same effect as our disco does today.

After the Charleston came the Apache dance. This dance was a dance of the common people from the villages who were in the factories. The male was dominant and he led the female partner around like a rug. It was considered much too vulgar to be accepted on the social scene. It traveled into the theatre for a brief stage career.

On its heels came the Tango. This dance was a folk

dance of Buenos Aires. Man's dominance once again became strong. It was polished and embraced by the fashion industry. Elegant attire led this dance onto the ballroom floor. The tango opened the door for a new profession - the exhibition dancer or the social dance instructors. The professional "gigolo" appears, a dance instructor with poor moral standards and character. The male image in dance once again dropped below God's standard.

The Flamenco folk dance birthed by Spanish folk art was strictly rhythmic. This effect, part gypsy, came from Andalusia. The dance of heel and foot work became popular in the forties and fifties. About 1956, men in dance began to rise again.

CONTEMPORARY PERIOD
(1800 - Present)

New philosophies toward intellectual freedom are wide open. Mass production, factories, and mechanical development have brought about the "abundant living" syndrome. Art and culture take a back seat to money and the driving force to get ahead. Everything is copy-cat. We dress alike, dance alike and read what everyone else is reading. It is the "let's keep up with the Joneses" era in America. Puritan influences spurned dance socially and spiritually. Joyous expression again fell into a ritualistic pattern and social dance was completely out of the picture.

In European countries dance grew in folk communities and churches. In the early 1800's, at the Cathedral in Seville, a group of six dancers (later increased to ten) danced regularly before the high altar. They were selected by the highest authority in the church and appointed to the responsibility of singing responses and dancing before the high altar. They would march in, drop to their knees and wait as the congregation grew quiet. The organ music would begin and they would sing a very melodious song and dance. They sometimes used castanets and were always dressed wonderfully. Their dance lasted about fifteen minutes and always caused a very deep reverence in the congregation. They wore different colors for different occasions. Choristers were always dressed to display the part needed for the theme of the service. Sometimes as a soldier, other times as a shepherd or pilgrim. On some occasions these dances were done with a complete orchestra.

Another cathedral in Toledo in the 18th century also had this type of a group. These dancers wore long white robes, belted at the waist with a broad stole or yoke. This garment was to represent the priesthood yoke. Low white shoes were worn as they danced.

Some of the important duties listed by the parishes of the town of Leon was to select and equip a number of young ladies for the sacred dance. They had four groups of twelve girls aged twelve and up. These girls learned first the processionals then the circle dances. After they were finished they filed into the middle of the choir where they sang.

The people of Romania were converted to Christianity by the Greek Orthodox Church. This church encouraged dance as part of worship. Dance became a common mode of expression at church festivals and is still very active today.

Spain also has dancing in the church for sacred purposes. This came about during the 11th-13th century when the kings restored dance to the church by lifting the ban.

Luxemburg used the processional, sanctioned by the Pope, for healing purposes. In a Paris dictionary of the 1800's the procession is described as a "moving chorus advancing in harmony." Many processions were preceeded by the cross, banners, flags and lighted candles. All dances during these days were done by appointed dancers.

We have touched on sacred dance throughout the world. There is no question dance has always been a part of worship and praise unto God; however, towards the close of the 18th century dance once again became banned by the churches because of indecent form and improper music at church carnivals and festivals. Since its purpose became distorted, it became mere symbolism and lost its authority.

America had the slim beginnings of sacred dance. The

South saw the rise of folk dance along with the West. The Shaker faith in 1825 used dance as part of their service. They came over from England which is where they probably were exposed to sacred dance. They believed dance was an important part of purification. Drama presentations had a highly esteemed purpose in the church and these people were very demonstrative and dramatic in nature. Men and women were separate when they danced and the young and old joined in. History books on dance contain pictures of these groups of people as well as others.

The Methodist church used processions in the early 1900's for pageants and festivals. Dance, for a number of reasons failed in these early years to meet the needs of everyday people.

1)   As the dancers failed to communicate their message, people naturally lost interest and didn't care to watch or participate. Dance must have a central purpose or theme and if it doesn't most people cannot relate to it. This was a sign of our contemporary age; distortion, abstracts, no absolute values, "modern art." You lose your people if they aren't relating to what you are doing.

2)   A lack of interest in dance or music in general had real influence during these years. Athletics and modern commercialism took much of everyone's time.

3)   Spiritual and moral decay caused dance to spiral downward. People enjoy dance when there is an experience involved. This is true in the natural realm as well as the spiritual. If technique and themes lose contact with life, people cannot grasp onto them. Movement as a medium of expression has become lost. Dance has become an unsettled form of art. There is proof dance will linger, yet it will struggle unless restored.

During the 1906 Pentecostal revival, the church world was shaken by what she saw; people dancing and rejoicing at the power and outpouring of the Holy Spirit. This is where we got our term "dancing in the Spirit." To the fundamental church this was offensive and certainly not of God. Other revivals had been stirring but this one so exploded it spread across America. True joy born by experiences of God came forth. This was a very emotional revival and the fundamental church rejected it as a manifestation of the flesh.

With the 1948 revival came the revelation of worship and praise contained in David's Tabernacle This also brought church government and divine order to the body of Christ. Restoration is a progressive step toward the coming of Christ. It brings into order and purpose all that God has done for centuries within the church. It brought the release of worship and praise, the revelation of the word of God, and the release of body ministry. There has continued to be an outpouring of the Holy Spirit ever since, with the charismatic renewal in 1950, along with the Jesus people visitation in the late 60's and early 70's. The charismatic renewal began to sweep rejoicing into denominational and Catholic churches. Each new visitation brings us closer to the plan of the glorious church. We must keep that vision burning.

Today dance is more readily being accepted in many churches. Denominational churches call it choir movement or drama. More liberal churches call it choreography and pageantry. Restoration churches call it Dance and recognize it as a ministry unto the Lord. Many churches have companies of dancers who minister in these areas. God intended His people to worship and praise Him. The Dance will grow in purpose and function as traditional bondages are broken.

III

DANCE AND THE CHURCH

Well documented notes, books and additional sources have given us a clear picture of dance history. From its earliest form there is an unbroken thread of dance. By examining the types of dance we see a social correlation. Dance is the expression of its age.

Dance had its beginning in the first civilization. We know that dance has always been a part of every culture on earth. All nations use music and dance and many believe that both are of divine origin. Musical instruments were being made from the first account in *Genesis Chapter 4*. Among those using early instruments are Syria and Egypt *(Genesis 31:27)*, the eastern nations *(Job 21:12)*, the Canaanites, Greeks, Chinese, Sumerians, Persians, Babylonians and Assyrians.

The rhythmical structure of dance and its design or pattern were documented as far back as the Egyptian Dynasty and early Greek nations. We will see that dance has always been essential and vital as a form of worship to heathen as well as God's people. We have no historical pictures or sources concerning Jewish dancing because the people of God were commanded not to make any graven images. We can however look to God's Word, the Bible, and to history books for knowledge concerning the dance in Israel.

Weighty religious ritual and legalism eventually robbed man of the liberty to rejoice in worship. The church allowed no dance due to social distortion and kept such activity out of her midst.

PRIMITIVE MAN
(Pre-Noah)

Primitive man danced to acknowledge love, war, acts of strength, food, health and worship. Many of his dances were in the order of mime or interpretation. If he needed rain, he would dance a rain dance. It wasn't until later in history that the dance was used for entertainment purposes.

Early man had a very basic passion for rhythm. He danced for love, before warfare, and during harvest. Religion was his life and there was no separation between dance for natural purposes and dance for spiritual purposes. Every aspect of life was unto God.

The three main groups of dances were love, war and religious ceremony. We will find these established themes permeating history. Imitative dances of nature were common. Movements consisted of stamping, clapping, swaying, shouting, crying and chanting. Noise always accompanied the dance and inspired corresponding movement.

An Egyptian drawing shows a burial dance of solemn procession done to the accompaniment of a choir and musicians. The picture shows stamping of feet while the choir beats out the rhythm with their hands. These drawings were found on cave walls done by early hunters and planters of cave dwellers. Some fragmented vases have also been found with the early dancing forms on them. As mentioned before, primitive man danced for:

1.   Love and worship
2.   Harvest
3.   War

As man gave himself to his god, the dance was a sign of total surrender.

ANCIENT MAN
Abraham - Ezra (1952 - 400 B.C.)

As we move on to ancient man, we will examine dance

from Abraham to a period shortly after Nehemiah. We see that separation between natural and spiritual has come about. The reason for this is the standard God has set for his people through the commandments and later the tabernacle. Heathen influence hurts Israel as she tries to attain that standard; evidenced in the story about the dance around the golden calf *(Exodus 32: 17-18).* We can compare this chapter to the previous chapter in *Exodus 15:21* where we see the story of Miriam's great dance of divine order and victory for her people.

The types of dance we see during this time period are processions, festival dance, celebratory dance, dance for weddings, funeral dance, the dance of victory, dance for warfare and ritualistic dance. Some of these victory dances were danced by all the people yet the greeting of the "victor" was done only by the closest relative. That's why Miriam led the women. That's where Michal should have greeted David, and also where Jephthah's daughter came to greet her father in dances. The festive dances were in honor of the particular national feast of Israel. Some of these dances were done with great joy. The Jewish dance also contained movements of spontaneity, i.e. David dancing before the Lord with all his might.

During this time, music and dance were placed under the guidance of the Tabernacle and the Priests. King David's Tabernacle brought order according to divine appointment. It is in David's Tabernacle where we find our choir, our worship leader, our orchestra leader, our expressive worshippers, and our ushers. King David took off his kingly garments and clothed himself as a priest. Then he began to worship and dance before the Lord.

> *"And David was clothed with a robe of fine linen, and all the Levites that bare the ark, and the singers, and Chenaniah, the master of the song with singers: David also had upon him an ephod of linen. Thus all Israel brought up the ark of the covenant of the Lord with shouting, and with sound of the cornet, and with trumpets, and with cymbals, making a noise with psalteries*

and harps. And it came to pass, as the ark of the covenant of the Lord came to the city of David, that Michal the daughter of Saul looking out at a window saw king David dancing and playing: and she despised him in her heart."

I Chronicles 15:27-29

Dancers danced to Psalms sung by the choir and accompanied by the musicians. The word "Selah", found in the Psalms means much more than "pause and consider what was just sung or played." It means "to pause, to set for a mood change, wait and meditate while there was a visual demonstration," possibly a dance if you please, of what was previously sung.

Anytime Israel would gather together, dance could be found in her midst. She was a dancing nation. A whole city would take part. The young and old were found dancing together. There are many scripture references for all these areas. Even at times of digging wells, all would gather around and sing "Spring up oh well. . ."

"Then Israel sang this song, Spring up O well; sing ye unto it."

Numbers 21:17

With the development of the temple and the priesthood, all worship centered around that location. The temple was subsequently destroyed and most singers and musicians carried away into Babylonian captivity. The second temple built by Zerubbabel around 520 B.C. became a restored house of worship. Temple worship was restored and *Nehemiah 12:31* refers to the great procession upon the walls.

"Then I brought up the princes of Judah upon the wall, and appointed two great companies of them that gave thanks, whereof one went on the right hand upon the wall toward the dung gate: And the other company of them that gave thanks went over against them, and I

after them, and the half of the people upon the wall, from beyond the tower of the furnaces even unto the broad wall."

Nehemiah 12:31 & 38

Note: The word "thanks" in scripture here means:

1. An extension of the hands
2. A choir or worshippers with hands lifted up
3. A sacrifice of praise

The Chaldeans used dance as a means of education to teach astronomy and science. They developed ballets to teach timing and ritual.

The Babylonians and Assyrians led in the development of harps and drums. They used men to dance more often and their women were dancing temple priestesses. The Egyptians' dance was their chief medium of religious expression. They developed dramas as a teaching tool and their youth were educated by dancing. They used trained dancers just as David did.

The Hebrew dances were very athletic in structure. They were done by chorus. The military used dance as a means of training. These people danced as David, with finesse and freedom. They danced to a choir and musicians. The dance was highly respected in Israel. At this time dance was no longer totally connected with everyday activities.

History describes for us Greek traveling dancers who used this movement as a means of healing. They would offer to dance around the sick in the form of a circle or ring dance. They claimed the power to cure all disease, including mental illness.

Music rose in intensity and became rich in meaning. Poetry became a beautiful mode of expression. Dance became moderate in movement with more emphasis on meaning. Dance grew into a highly esteemed art. Kings were dancing, prophets were dancing, armies were dancing, everyone danced!

NEW TESTAMENT AGE
Birth of Christ - Dark Ages (30 A.D. - 500 A.D.)

Slowly, after the destruction of the second temple, temple worship began to fall. Ezra had set up many synagogues in Israel when the land was returned to the Jews. These meeting places were designed to meet the needs of the whole family. A place of teaching, and a place of worship. But with time, idolatry, apostasy, and unbelief penetrated God's people. Worship was allowed to degenerate into formalism. The joyful spontaniety of David was gone. Eventually the temple was destroyed and rebuilt under Herod.

This was a balanced time period. The faithful carried on with zeal and enjoyed festive times with other believers. The influence of the Saducees and Pharisees caused joyful worship to degenerate into ritual; but God always prepares a remnant to worship Him in Spirit and truth.

Jesus was outspoken concerning the formalism and hypocrisy of His time. He condemned worship and praise that was devoid of heart-felt love and adoration for God. He never repudiated Old Testament vocal or instrumental music and dance. Paul thanked God he worshipped in the manner of the Old Testament fathers:

> *"But this I confess unto thee, that after the way which they call heresy, so worship I the God of my fathers, believing all things which are written in the law and in the prophets."*
>
> *Acts 24:14*

These New Testament believers continually turned to the Psalms and Prophets in their praise, preaching, and teaching. Worship and praise regained strength until the third century. Temple worship reaches its peak during feast days around 40 A.D. We have record of half a million devout Jews flowing into Jerusalem three times a year to worship God during the feast. It was at one of these times, Pentecost, that the early church was born. Paul exhorts the early church to worship God with Psalms, hymns and spiritual songs.

> *"Let the word of Christ dwell in you richly in all wisdom; teaching and admonishing one another in psalms, hymns and spiritual songs, singing with grace in your hearts to the Lord."*
>
> *Colossians 3:16*

In *Acts 6:5* Prochorus was chosen to be a deacon. A study of this man's name reveals his ministry: a leader of the dance. His function was worship leader who also led in the round dance.

Jesus exhorted his disciples to leap for joy when darkness or persecution became stronger.

> *"Rejoice ye in that day, and leap for joy: for, behold, your reward is great in heaven: for in the like manner did their fathers unto the prophets."*
>
> *Luke 6:23*

Jesus also likened that generation unto a generation who did not dance when music was played.

> *"They are like unto children sitting in the market place, and calling one to another, and saying, we have piped unto you, and ye have not danced; we have mourned to you and ye have not wept."*
>
> *Luke 7:32*

In the parable of the prodigal son, we see dancing was a joyous pastime of the people.

> *"Now his elder son was in the field and as he came and drew nigh to the house, he heard music and dancing."*
>
> *Luke 15:25*

One traditional Jewish worship dance was done to

Psalms 118:27. It began with a procession which would then end around the altar. *Ezekiel 6:11* was also a traditional dance of the Jews. Many danced in open fields during the seasons of planting and sowing. They also danced at the digging of wells.

The Christian church celebrated their God. He moved among them in power and might with signs and wonders.

Early Christian dances were described as heavenly joys, and a part of the adoration of the divine Jesus Christ done by angels and saints. The angels could sing and dance the joy of creation but only the saint can participate in the joy of creation as well as the praise of redemption. This may be the underlying reason so many recorded facts of visions are concerned with saints and angels together praising God.

Andrew, while being martyred said, "release my body in order that my soul, dancing with angels may praise thee." We understand that it is our privilege to dance before God with the angels, by the power of salvation, and even Jesus joins in with us *(Zephaniah 3:17):*

> *"The Lord thy God in the midst of thee is mighty: he will save, he will rejoice over thee with joy; he will rest in his love, he will joy over thee with singing."*

Around 300 A.D., the type of music done in the church consisted of three types:

1. Direct psalmody (singing of the Psalms);
2. Responsive psalmody (a soloist leads while the congregation sings amen or alleluia); and,
3. Antiphonal psalmody (alternating half choruses).

It was Paul's task to align the Greek churches to Christian doctrine. The Greek culture had a great influence on the early church. The Greeks loved body, soul and self. Dance became a highly developed art and many were personally trained concerning its use. The Greek Phalanx was led by a musician to battle. The commanders in the battle were called principle dancers. According to ancient writings the men who danced best were the best warriors. David certainly is an example of this. Instruments gave the signal for attack and the rhythm and sound determined the motion and intensity of the fighting warriors. Great warriors ordered their marching steps according to the sound they heard. A great example of this principle for the church is how the Lord instructed Jehosaphat to lead the people into war. *"With the singers and dancers and instruments going before the army." (I Chronicles 20).*

Rome began to rise to power and impose upon the church. The Romans were great imitators, cruel and idolatrous. Their dance for worship was brutal and sensual. At this time some church leaders began to ban the dance as a form of praise because of the Roman influence. Under Nero the Christians were persecuted strongly. The Romans loved the dance just as the Greeks did, but it was used for totally wrong purposes.

After the fall of the Grecian Roman culture, the Christians began to transform the Roman Empire into a Christian Empire. Eventually Constantine's church organization in 313 A.D. led to ritual, formalism and fewer expressions of joy or spontaneous praise.

We have some historial exhortations by early church fathers who longed to once again see singing and rejoicing as a means of expression unto God:

Clement of Alexandria (215 A.D.) - "I will show you the word and the mysteries of the word and describe them for you as an image of your own fate. This is the mountain beloved of God, Zion, and on it rejoice God's daughters, the most beautiful lambs which reveal the reverent festival of the word to the accompaniment of constantly repeated choral dancing. By righteousness, man may partake in them also. The song is a holy hymn to the King of all creation. Oh in truth, Holy mysteries, oh what pure light whilst torches are born before me, I perceive the heavens and the Lord. I am led into the service of God. I become sanctified, thou also if thou wishest mayest let theyself be led. Then shalt thou dance in a ring dance, together with the angels around Him who is without beginning or end."

Chrysostom (386 A.D.) - ". . .of those in heaven, those on earth a unison is made, one general assembly, one single service of thanksgiving, one single transport of rejoicing, one joyous dance."

Ambrose (387 A.D.) - Encouraged the people to once again sing hymns and psalms.

Ambrose (390 A.D.) - "Everything is right when it springs from the fear of the Lord. Let's dance as David did. Let's not be ashamed to show adoration of God. Dance uplifts the body above the earth into the heavenlies. Dance bound up with faith is a testimony to the living grace of God. He who dances as David danced, dances in grace."

Augustine (394 A.D.) - "Let's keep the sacred dances, discipline is most severe."

Ambrose (400 A.D.) - "And just as he who dances with his body rushing through the rotating movements of the limbs, acquires a right to share in the round dance, in the same way he who dances the spiritual dance, always moving in the ecstasy of faith, acquires a right to dance in the ring of all creation."

St. Basil (4th Century) - "Could there be anything more blessed than to imitate on earth the ring dance of the angels, and at dawn to raise their voices in prayer, and by hymns, and songs to glorify the rising Creator?"

Because of third century persecution of the church, the praise and worship became less spontaneous. Constantine set up a church state with rules and regulations. Confusion over using the psalms of David or humanly composed hymns stirred.

The psalmody and chant became the expression of just a few. Jerome of 340-420 A.D. began to warn the church of becoming a theatre with its music and dance. The synod of Laodocia in 343-381 ruled that none should sing in church except those regularly appointed singers. The joy of singing, spontaneous dancing, rejoicing with clapping and audible praise were heard by only a few. The sacred procession is still found along with the singing of psalms and hymns. By an accurate account of services held in Jerusalem around 394 A.D., we still see early church life and some form of liturgical worship. Almost every service is opened with a processional along with antiphonal singing. The churches were sometimes decorated with banners and flags which were used to accentuate the pomp surrounding their celebration.

With the apostles of the early church gone, the prophetic voice gone, the anointing brought by worship and praise gone, the church was about to enter the dark ages. Voices of the early church fathers were still trying to exhort the people to cry out to God.

Theodoret (430 A.D.) - "I see dance as a virtue in harmony with power from above."

Many problems began to lead the church down that pathway through the dark ages. Because of a state-organized church everyone had to belong. She received all kinds of people and as a result of sin and impurity, attitudes and motives of the heart went unchallenged. At feast days, men and women began to dance together, dances were being executed by women with frivolous and indecent movements. Unsuitable songs were being sung to accompany these dances.

DARK AGES
(550 - 1500)

Greek philosophy has failed, Roman unity has gone and both the Greek and Egyptian religions have been consumed by Christianity. The church has now become the universal power and transferred her seat of authority to Europe. Religion has become everything to everybody. Every man and woman was commanded to be a member of the State Church. This church became the controlling force of life. It brought in the feudal system, social organization, and it was evident that everyone submitted to the common good, no matter what it was.

Now we begin to see men and women dancing together. These dances began to use frivolous and indecent movements. The accompanying music was demoralizing. Plays and drama centered around evil vs. light, spirituality and carnality, mind and body, evil and good intent. These elements infected the people and distorted doctrinal truths. Distortion was evident everywhere. Anything giving pleasure to the body was considered evil and thought to be wicked. The body was even punished and bruised to exert the soul; therefore dance, because it was pleasurable and physical, was frowned upon in all forms. Only the occasional ritual dance was left. This brought division between the people and the church. Most churches completely banned the dance along with most music. Because of drunkenness at church festivals, social or folk dance was also stopped. Superstitions, black death and the mania epidemics were formulated during this time. The rise of a death complex, religious fanaticism, sensuality, and war continued to bring darkness over this time period. Soon, many people were overrun with mental illness, famine and pestilence. Foundations in the word of God were shaken. Witchcraft rose in popularity and a demonical dancing epidemic caused by the Black Death scare totally twisted all principles.

As the church darkened people began looking for expression elsewhere. Thus began the rise of court dances and social balls. Great cathedrals and universities were being built. A desire for increased knowledge and the expansion of trade led to the rise of common laymen attaining knighthood. Barbaric conditions of life which led to the ban of dance in the church promoted dance outside the church. Elaborate masquerade balls and court dances were seen in all the courts of the land. Half-secular, half-morality dramas and plays were on the rise.

Growth in hierarchy among the clergy and the institutionalized function of the church caused much displeasure. Liturgical worship functioned at the call of the bishop. Bishop Gregory (540-604 A.D.) proclaimed singing as a clerical function. Only in the small meetings of the remnant did joy, worship and praise live on continually. Here are some quotes from church fathers still calling for truth:

Bishop of Milan - (600 A.D.) "Dance as David."

St. Gregory of Nazianzus - (600 A.D.) "Dance as David to true refreshment of the Ark which I consider to be the approach to God, the swift encircling steps in the manner of the mystery."

Abbot Meletius-(700 A.D.) "I like the church procession

around the altar with the choir."

Because of so much dance in the early Catholic Church, rules were set down by the Bishop concerning who would dance when. The church dances became known as the sacred dance and the festive dance. Each was danced by separate people.

SACRED	FESTIVE
Priest	No clergy
Bishop	All congregation
Monks	Children
Nuns	
Choir Boys	

During the eleventh and twelfth centuries, churches in Wales used the procession during their services. England began to use some congregational dance in the fourteenth century. Spanish kings renewed the dance in their church. Catholic priests allowed dance during the 1300's, but it became sensual, out of order and filled with drunkenness in 1544, and was banned once again.

The Dark Ages left the church dead. The Holy Spirit was not received in churches built to worship man.

THE RENAISSANCE
(1500 - 1700)

A new order in the "church" and state begins to be revealed during the Renaissance. There is a drive to establish education for the wealthy. Seeking personal satisfaction is the rule. This led to creativity and new expression in song and dance. Creativity flows from the people as well as the clergy. Dance instruction and vast improvements in music stirs new respect for these areas. It is the age of the rebirth of the arts. Interest in technique gains strength.

There was a great division between the social court dance and the sacred dance. Ballet developed and grew in popularity but allowed no room for free expression. Spontaniety was lost.

The folk dance was developed joyously. The common people loved to dance, and their dance had purpose. Court dances were void of purpose, formal and strictly ordered. It became a sign of social esteem if one was established as a dancer and schooled in professional and social dance. The first ballet school was established during this time period. The ballets continued to use the three central themes of dance: worship, warfare and harvest. Dance became a tool for entertainment and ballet held the strictest attention. Dance was not joyful or flowing. Only the folk dances and some dance in the church retained a spirit of rejoicing. Because all the nobility danced, the common people danced even more. They had a total freedom to express their love for life and praise to their God. All ages joined in the fun because these dances did not demand great skill. The people expressed joy and sorrow through dances carried down from generation to generation.

As God breathed again upon the church, pagan superstitions died out, but a new stream arose - mythology. Spiritual themes of idolatry and Greek mythology became the basis for entertainment. This is a spiritual principle easily recognized. Whenever God moves in real restoration, Satan comes on the scene with a counterfeit. As the Lord rained new light on the churches by restoring song, dance and joy, the theatres counter balanced the rain.

Songs of joy, laughter and rhythm began to be heard in the church. Dance processions had a lighter step with color and expression. Circle dances with chorus were joyfully danced. Triumphant church hymns rang out with truth and dignity. These were born out of experience and readily accepted from God's hand.

One of the most documented dances of this time period was called the Dance of Death. This dance was commonly practiced at death beds everywhere. As the offering was prepared, the dance moved around the death bed, and the choir would sing and stamp their feet, beating out rhythm. After this dance was finished the priest would come and minister.

This dance was not one of great mourning, but one of lighter spirit. Dances of this nature are common throughout history. God promises to turn our mourning into dancing.

The Dark Ages brought ritual dance into the church; dances of strict religiosity in the form of works. Even Martin Luther moving towards the vision the Lord gave him of justification by faith, used to take part in the beating of his flesh. This was a procession common to the Flagellants of 1200 A.D. The plague and sin could be driven out of a body by a procession, led by the cross and church standards, while men beat or scourged themselves. They were labeled "brethren of the cross." As truth and revelation were restored to the church, these practices disappeared. Soon the Roman church and the Protestant church split.

At the close of the 17th century, God moved again. This was the beginning of the Holiness movement. God expected more truth about living a Christian life to be discerned. John Wesley was the forerunner during this time period. He taught principles of prayer and a separated life unto Christ. Many new believers walked through the door of this restored truth into newness of life.

IV

THE PURPOSE OF RESTORATION

Restoration is simply taking what is God's in the first place, using it for His glory, and giving it back to Him. Dance began in the heavenlies by the creation of God. Lucifer's fall corrupted its purity. We are regaining control of the arts and using them to worship Jesus. God is going to restore all things that belonged to Him from the beginning - those things spoken by the Holy prophets:

> ". . .And he shall send Jesus Christ which before was preached unto you: whom the heaven must receive (retain) until the times of restitution of all things, which God hath spoken by the mouth of all his holy prophets since the world began."
>
> Acts 3:20-21

This wonderful message of restoration makes the Christian life so exciting! There is so much for God's Church to do, so much ground to recover in the name of Jesus. It is God's intention to restore, otherwise he would have created an ugly mess. He created beautifully and completely, now the church must cry "Restore!"

> "But this is a people robbed and spoiled; they are all of them snared in holes, and they are hid in prison houses: they are for a prey and none delivereth; for a spoil, and

none saith RESTORE. Who among you will give ear to this? Who will hearken and hear for the time to come?"
                                                     Isaiah 42:22-23

"And I will restore to you the years that the locust hath eaten, the cankerworm, and the caterpillar, and the palmerworm, my great army which I sent among you."
                                                           Joel 2:25

"And they that shall be of thee shall build the old waste places: thou shalt raise up the foundations of many generations; and thou shalt be called, The repairer of the breach, The restorer of paths to dwell in."
                                                        Isaiah 58:12

So we may know the story of Lucifer's (Satan) fall to earth and his work of corruption, let's go back to his first place of authority. *Isaiah 14:12-17* tells us about it:

"How art thou fallen from heaven, O Lucifer, son of the morning! how art thou cut down to the ground, which didst weaken the nations! For thou hast said in thine heart, I will ascend into heaven, I will exalt my throne above the stars of God: I will sit also upon the mount of the congregation, in the sides of the north: I will ascend above the heights of the clouds; I will be like the most High. Yet thou shalt be brought down to hell, to the sides of the pit. They that see thee shall narrowly look upon thee, and consider thee, saying, Is this that man that made the earth tremble, that did shake the kingdoms; that made the word as a wilderness, and destroyed the cities thereof; that opened not the house of his prisoners?"

We can see that our work is cut out for us. There is more to salvation then going to heaven. Lucifer wanted to be like God. He is still trying to set up his own kingdom on earth, but that kingdom of darkness is to be overthrown by the Kingdom of Light. God wants us to rise up and begin His work of restoration!

What was Lucifer's position in Heaven? He was to cover God's throne with praise and worship.

> *"Thou hast been in Eden the garden of God; every precious stone was thy covering, the sardius, topaz, and the diamond, the beryl, the onyx, and the jasper, the sapphire, the emerald and the carbuncle, and gold: the workmanship of thy tabrets and of thy pipes was prepared in thee in the day that thou was created. Thou art the anointed cherub that covereth; and I have set thee so: thou wast upon the holy mountain of God; thou hast walked up and down in the midst of the stones of fire. Thou wast perfect in thy ways from the day that thou was created, till iniquity was found in thee."*
>
> *Ezekiel 28:13-15*

Lucifer was the leader of the heavenly choir who sang at the dawn of creation. His anointed ministry was to cover God's throne with worship and praise. He was clothed as a priest with all precious stones, and he had the workmanship of all tabrets (rhythm), pipes (harmony), and viols (melody), in him on the day he was created.

Lucifer rebelled and was cast down to earth. Because of his ability merely to duplicate what he saw in heaven, divine harmony was broken. All forms of music, dance, and song have been corrupted and only when performed with a heart that worships God are they restored unto His name. Lucifer's ability to establish them on earth is only with distortion and vainglory. Worldly dance and music are especially corrupt. We must remember that music and dance are not the culprits; but motivation cf the heart. The tools of music and dance now have the power to destory, corrupt, incite and degrade the human body, soul and spirit.

We are seeing in the midst of the church something that goes beyond the charismatic renewal. We are seeing restoration!

God moves in, shakes up, strips down, cleans up and gives back beauty, glory, power and honor. It is much more than renewing.All dominion, power and glory were given to the believers - God's Church - after the resurrection of Christ. God is moving beyond our need to be blessed and is preparing us to rule and reign with dominion over all His creation.

There is so much to deal with in this area I cannot cover it all here; I will limit myself to the areas of worship and praise. We are involved with three principles of restoration:

A.   Recovery of divine principles.
B.   Recovery of spiritual life.
C.   Completion and fulfillment of God's plan.

(Please note chart on following page.)

We see the area of worship and praise in church history was established with David, flourished with Solomon, and was restored under Joash, Hezekiah, Josiah, Zerubbabel and Nehemiah. The New Testament church continued to worship and praise God as David instructed until the end of the third century. We look at some churches today and worship and praise is absent. That is why God said He would restore David's Tabernacle. This will be Jesus' "Welcome Home" celebration. Let's welcome Him with much music and dance! The Bride always danced to greet her Bridegroom, and as He approached she rejoiced even more.

In order to understand the new we must understand the old. The Old Testament is our pattern to be applied to the New Testament and Jesus Christ. I would like to list Old Testament forms of worship listed in David's Tabernacle and correlate New Testament scriptures:

WORSHIP	OLD	NEW
Song	I Chron. 15:16-27	Col. 3:16
Instruments	I Chron. 25:1-7	Eph. 5:18-19
Recordings	I Chron. 16:4	Rev. 1:10-11
Thanking	I Chron. 16:4, 8	I Thess. 5:18
Praise	I Chron. 16:4, 36	Heb. 13:15

DAVID'S TABERNACLE

A. Recovery of Divine Principles	B. Recovery of Spiritual Life	C. Recover and Establish God's Plan On Earth
1. God's Throne is seat of Ultimate Authority *Psalms 89:14*	1. Priesthood of the Believer *I Peter 2:9*	1. Jesus given Throne of His father David *Luke 1:31-33*
2. Church shall cover the Throne with praise and worship *Psalms 78:67-72*	2. Enter into His Presence *Psalms 100:1-5*	2. Government of peace, joy, judgement *Isaiah 9:6-7*
3. God inhabits the praises of His people *Psalms 22:3*	3. Spiritual sacrifices *Hebrews 13:15; Psalms 107:22*	3. Build again the Tabernacle of David *Acts 15:16*
4. Worship in Spirit and Truth *John 4:21-24*	4. Deliverance *Obadiah 17, 21*	4. Come Unto Zion *Hebrews 12:18-24*
5. Due order and judgement *Psalms 16:5*	5. Created to praise *Psalms 102:16-20*	5. His house established forever *Isaiah 2:3-4*

Levitical Praise	*I Chron. 16:37*	*Heb. 6:19-20; 10: 19-21*
Psalm Singing	*I Chron. 16:7*	*James 5:13; I Cor. 14:26*
Joy & Rejoicing	*I Chron. 16:10, 27, 31*	*Acts 13:52*
Clapping	*Psalm 47:1*	
Shout	*I Chron. 15:28*	*I Thess. 14:16*
Dance	*Psalm 149:3*	*Luke 15:25*
Lifting of Hands	*Psalm 134:2*	*I Tim. 2:8*
Bowing worship	*I Chron. 16:29*	*John 12:3*
Seek the Lord	*I Chron. 16:10-11*	*Acts 15:17*
Spiritual Sacrifices	*Psalm 27:6, 116:17*	*I Peter 2:3-5*
Amen blessing	*I Chron. 16:36*	*I Cor. 14:16*

The work of restoration will be revealed in seven areas: truth will unfold, *III John 4;* ministries will function in the body of Christ, *Ephesians 4:11-16;* the people will be restored with joy and healing, *Isaiah 66:14;* worship and praise will be completely lifted from the heart and not ritualistic, *Jeremiah 31:12-13;* years of sowing toil, hard work and desert experiences will be reaped. We will receive time to do again what God commands us to do, *Joel 2:25;* we will be instructed in righteousness and have sure paths to dwell in, *Isaiah, 58:12;* the kingdom of God shall be revealed in the earth, *I Corinthians 15:24.* [5]

Part of restoration is creating a dwelling place for the presence of the Lord. The ark of the Lord in the Old Testament was a throne or seat of God's manifest presence. This was where God revealed His fullness, His power, His presence and His glory. David wanted to bring the ark out of the camp of the Philistines and back to Jerusalem. He needed a dwelling place of the ark so he built the tabernacle. David consulted with the leaders and the people. They agreed the ark should be brought to Jerusalem. So David gathered the people together and put the ark on a new cart. Uzza and Ahio drove the cart

---

5 Present Day Truths, K.R. Iverson, Portland, Oregon

and all of Israel danced and rejoiced as the cart traveled along. Then, when they came to the threshing floor of Chidon, Uzza put forth his hand to steady the ark because the oxen stumbled, and he was struck dead by God. This upset David and stopped the joyous procession for three months. During this period, David sought God as to how he should bring in the ark of God. It is in *I Chronicles chapter fifteen* that David prepared a place for the ark of God. Then David said that none should carry the ark but the Levites or priests. They are the ones God set to minister unto Him forever. God smote Uzza the first time because, "Philistine-ly," the people put the ark on a new cart. The next time David assembled the priests and Levites and commanded them to sanctify themselves to bring up the ark. *"For because ye did it not at the first, the Lord was angry because we sought Him not after His due order."*

As all Israel brought the ark into Jerusalem, David appointed singers and players of instruments, removed his kingly garments, dressed as a priest and led the dancing. Once the ark was set up in the midst of the Tabernacle, David appointed Levites to minister before the Lord.

It is so important for us to glean from these chapters the due order. We are not advocating a church dancing freely with no divine order or structure. God does not want this. The key of David to unlock the door for all Gentiles to enter into God's Presence is divine order. There is no veil to hide God's glory in this Tabernacle. All who draw nigh unto God may see it.

As worshippers sit in your church each Sunday, deep within their spirit is the ark of God's presence. It is the job of every leader to cause the people to bring up that ark. We must cause the very presence of God to stir within us until the presence of God glows out of our innermost beings like a river, bathing those around us in life. Praise is the tool that causes us to physically and spiritually respond to the work of the Lord. As we send up this burnt offering or vapor of praise and worship, we create an atmosphere for God to come into our midst and move with signs and wonders. If God's manifest presence and power in our services is lacking, we have not created an atmosphere for Him. If you're a new church, or new to these ideas, concentrate on teaching your people to bring up the ark. Teach them how to release themselves to praise God. If you already have these principles at work, then you may begin to use them for tools of outreach. Work more on skill, special music or dances; perhaps dramas or choir choreography. If both are functioning well, set up a training program for children. Begin to teach them how to come into God's presence.

As we worship and praise God unashamedly and openly before all in faithful obedience to Him, He will begin to draw others into this communion. Jesus has opened the way for us by His blood, therefore His Presence is not limited to a few but to whosoever will come.

These days are fulfilling the law and the prophets. Every prophet in the Bible spoke about restoration. This was not some chance doctrine someone discovered, but it was written about in God's word from cover to cover.

Micah - gave the faithful remnant promises of restoration in Messianic age.

Zephaniah - comforted faithful remnant with promises of restoration.

Haggai - encouraged leaders doing work of restoration.

Zechariah - stirred the remnant to continue work of restoration.

Malachi - encouraged remnant to continue work of restoration. Rebuked leadership and people for formalizing temple worship.

Jeremiah - all disobedience to God's ways judged with captivity. After repentance, promise of restoration.

Ezekiel - restoration in times of Messiah. The glory returns to a new temple under a new covenant.

Daniel - "Prophet of Captivity" foresaw the kingdom of God grow on the earth.

Hosea - restoration through Messiah.

Joel - restoration through latter rain.

Amos - promise of restoration in Messianic age.

Obediah - promise of restoration and deliverance.

Once this vision surges inside you, it will set your heart aflame for the work of the Lord. Restoration through the Holy Spirit will be made manifest.

V

DANCE AS A PRIEST

Dance apart from God is exercise, but done by redeemed believers it is an act of worship. As our lives become wholly set apart unto God; sanctified and yielded to Him as an act of love, praise and worship cause us to be lifted into His presence. Worship is a lifestyle. Every moment of our lives should be spent praising our Lord.

> *"Ye also, as lively stones, are built up a spiritual house, an holy priesthood, to offer up spiritual sacrifices, acceptable to God by Jesus Christ."*
>
> *I Peter 2:5*

> *"But ye are a chosen generation, a royal priesthood, a holy nation, a peculiar people; that ye should show forth the praises of him who hath called you out of darkness into his marvelous light."*
>
> *I Peter 2:9*

These scriptures reveal to us that as believers in Jesus, we are to function as priests and offer sacrifices unto Him. Redemption through the cross brought a new covenant. No more animal sacrifices are necessary. Jesus Christ is our sacrifice; the Lamb of God. Many important lessons and commands are relegated to us concerning the priesthood of the believer. This is God's pattern that is unchangeable and gleaned from

Old Testament actualities.

There are two significant mountains in the Bible; Mt. Sinai and Mt. Zion. Contrasting these mountains we learn why God has chosen Zion.

> *"For ye are not come unto the mount that might be touched, and that burned with fire, not unto blackness, and darkness, and tempest, And the sound of a trumpet, and the voice of words; which voice they that heard entreated that the word should not be spoken to them any more: (For they could not endure that which was commanded, And if so much as a beast touch the mountain, it shall be stoned, or thrust through with a dart: And so terrible was the sight, that Moses said, I exceedingly fear and quake:) But ye are come unto mount Zion, and unto the city of the living God, the heavenly Jerusalem, and to an innumberable company of angels."*
>
> *Hebrews 12:18-22*

Mt. Sinai

a. Revelation of God's physical presence
b. Forbid to come near
c. Mt. of signs and wonders

Mt. Zion

a. Revelation of God's spiritual presence
b. Free access
c. Mt. of ways and modes of God's Spirit.

David chose Zion in which to place his tabernacle, his priests and his Levites.

> *"Who shall ascend into the hill of the Lord? Or who shall stand in his holy place? He that hath clean hands, and a pure heart; who hath not lifted up his soul unto vanity, nor sworn deceitfully."*
>
> *Psalms 24:3-4*

Our first separation as a Levite is our calling unto God. As a worshipper, we are to be a priest and Levite unto the Lord. The second requirements are clean hands and a pure heart. We must be cleansed and purified. We are Levites by virtue of bloodline. Clean and unclean don't get along in the spiritual realm. Jesus is our atonement for sin, thereby we have access unto the throne of Grace, His very presence.

> *"Let us draw near with a true heart in full assurance of faith, having our hearts sprinkled from an evil conscience, and our bodies washed with pure water."*
> *Hebrews 10:22*

This is only one reason why a congregation can participate in a dance of great joy, for He hath purchased for us salvation. He chose us to be the royal priesthood. We are to abandon ourselves in worship and praise unto Him.

> *"I beseech you therefore, brethren, by the mercies of God, that ye present your bodies a living sacrifice, holy, acceptable unto God, which is your reasonable service."*
> *Romans 12:1*

We are called because God has a purpose for each one of us. He chose us, we didn't choose Him. It isn't for our own ministry but for a part of the overall purpose of the Kingdom of God. By ministering as a priest, you become God's gift to the people. God makes sure that those chosen have the necessary gifts and abilities to carry out that function. We have everything we need in Jesus. Our ministry of dedication must be first UNTO Him before we attempt to minister FOR Him. If we aren't clean, yielded vessels it is impossible to sing, dance, preach or teach in the house of God for Jesus. The highest place of ministry is one that first ministers to Jesus then He in turn lets His presence and anointing come to us. His glory and blessing will then flow to all His people present. The presence of God's Kingdom being made manifest in the earth depends upon those who are obedient to keep the duties of a priest. By surrounding the Lord with praise and worship,

Heaven and Earth are joined.

> *"By him therefore let us offer the sacrifice of praise to God continually, that is, the fruit of our lips giving thanks to his name."*
>
> *Hebrews 13:15*

The third Levitical responsibility was to be separated, dedicated and consecrated. This area is where we prove ourselves faithful. We begin to learn of Him and His ways and as we are consecrated or sanctified then we may be commissioned to minister to His people. We must apply God's truth to our hearts every day. We want Jesus to so change us that when we dance before Him, sing before Him, or minister in any way before Him; He will draw nigh unto us with His anointing power. This period of time is very testing and tedious. Here is where many believers give up. Our lives should be above reproach. There must be no basis for a bad report. Worshipping Jesus requires a whole heart, HE WANTS ALL OF US! This is part of our foundation being laid that we may be built up in Jesus. We then in turn teach others by word and example the lifestyle set apart for God.

> *"And they shall teach my people the difference between the holy and profane, and cause them to discern between the unclean and the clean."*
>
> *Ezekiel 44:23*

Another requirement of a priest is that they wait on their office.

> *"And these are they whom David set over the service of song in the house of the Lord, after that the ark had rest. And they ministered before the dwelling place of the tabernacle of the congregation with singing, until Solomon had built the house of the Lord in Jerusalem: and then they waited on their office according to their order."*
>
> *I Chronicles 6:31-32*

> *"Or ministry, let us wait on our ministering: or he
> that teacheth, on teaching; Or he that exhorteth, on
> exhortation: he that giveth, let him do it with sim-
> plicity; he that ruleth, with diligence; he that showeth
> mercy, with cheerfulness."*
>
> *Romans 12:7-8*

To wait means we stand in ready to be used. It doesn't
mean we sit in the same pew Sunday after Sunday waiting for
God to sovereignly visit us from heaven with a word of direction. We are called or chosen, cleansed, consecrated and
dedicated to serve God, not wait forever to go to heaven.
There are too many beautiful Christians who have absolutely
no drive or zeal. They haven't done anything for God yet.
Get up and move in His power. We are all priests to praise.
Jesus made the provision for us, the key is believing and receiving that provision. Wait while doing; wait on God; serve
Him.

Another area of Levitical duty is rank and order; learning to flow in a position of service. As dancers we don't just
dance when we feel like it. The whole service must be taken
into consideration. God is a God of divine order. We must have
rank and order in the church. This is why we have leadership.
An example would be the order of the Levitical clan. With
4,000 appointed singers, dancers, and musicians, there had to
be order!

SINGERS, DANCERS, and MUSICIANS
RANK and ORDER

1. Were appointed by leadership - *I Chron. 16:9, 23;
   15:16-28.*
2. Were separated unto this work - *I Chron. 25:1.*
3. Were taught by those over them - *I Chron. 25:1-7;
   II Chron. 23:13.*
4. Were directed by leadership - *I Chron. 15:22, 27.*
5. Were placed in ranks - *I Chron. 15:16-18.*
6. Were chosen by name - *I Chron. 16:37-41* (personal

recognition.)

7. Were skillful - *I Chron. 15:22; II Chron. 34:12; Psalms 33:3.*
8. Were employed in their work - *I Chron. 9:22.*
9. Were responsible for praise - *I Chron. 6:31-32.*
10. Were waiting on office - *I Chron. 6:31-32; II Chron. 7:6; 35:15.*
11. Received their portion - *Neh. 7:1, 44, 73; 10:28; 13:5, 10.*
12. Functioned in their courses - *I Chron. 25:1-31.*

This is a very helpful pattern to follow as an example of rank and order. When we find where we fit we can link arms with those around us and with the strength of others we can move ahead into what God has called us to do. An army marches in order. One person can't do everything. We are the army of God - the Church of Jesus Christ!

After priests before the Lord are called, chosen, consecrated, dedicated, separated and commissioned by rank and order; they are given holy responsibility or charge. A ministry will flow that brings forth good fruit. God's presence in us will affect others. Only out of an inner experience can the truth of Jesus be applied to others. We are to lift up the standard so others may follow.

> *"Go through, go through the gates; prepare ye the way of the people; cast up, cast up the highway; gather out the stones; lift up a standard for the people."*
> *Isaiah 62:10*

Why is it that social dance has set the standard for the world to follow? Now Christians can restore that area to the church. The sanctuary will become the arena for the joy of the Lord. Technique and skill will be displayed to the world from the church schools and not ballet schools. Musicals and dramas will be attended by people who know they are going to be participants and not spectators. Jesus challenges us to know who we are worshipping and bring forth that relationship.

Only by a relationship with Him can we minister effectively in truth. You should be manifesting that relationship visibly.

The next area of Levitical ministry deals with clothing. Priests in the Old and New Testaments wore special garments. This is a natural truth that should be applied in a spiritual sense also.

> *"Also the Levites which were the singers, all of them of Asaph, of Heman, of Jeduthun, with their sons and their brethren, being arrayed in white linen, having cymbals and psalteries and harps, stood at the east end of the altar, and with them a hundred and twenty priests sounding with trumpets."*
>
> *II Chronicles 5:12*

We have applied this in the natural sense by clothing our choirs in robes. This is a correct scriptural premise, but I would like to examine being clothed in white linen in order to minister to the Lord.

> *"And thou shalt make holy garments for Aaron thy brother for glory and beauty."*
>
> *Exodus 28:2*

Each garment worn by a priest represents a spiritual truth. Aaron had to be properly clothed physically to come before the Lord, as we must be properly clothed spiritually. These garments were made once and man fit into them. They did not change to fit the man. God's truth does not change - we are the ones who must line up according to His word. We must take each garment of truth and not create our own. WE change, not the truth.

> *"Take Aaron and Eleazar his son, and bring them up unto mount Hor: And strip Aaron of his garments, and put them upon Eleazar his son: and Aaron shall be gathered unto his people, and shall die there."*
>
> *Numbers 20:25-26*

The garments were made for beauty and glory. Holy garments should naturally produce God's glory and beauty. The glory of God will naturally rest upon His garments of truth, while our own are as filthy rags. To be a candidate of the glory of God, we must be clothed in truth and righteousness. Holiness is produced by truth. To refuse truth is to refuse Christ and His provision for nakedness.

When the Lord gives an additional garment of truth, we do not discard the previous one but we maintain each truth and add to our spiritual wardrobe. With each new garment we move out of spiritual captivity. Our work of practical sanctification goes on continually. The more garments of truth we put on, the less flesh will be revealed.

Once we are clothed in His truth, He can pour upon us His anointing. Jesus is Truth, the more we have of Him the more joy, liberty, peace and love we have. We must be clothed in His garments, ready to minister before Him. As we live and walk in truth daily, we grow closer to Jesus.

As the priesthood of the believer continues to be unfolded we need to arise to each new level of consecration revealed. We all have access to the throne of God's presence through Jesus, but who will consecrate themselves to move into that Holy Place by applying the spiritual truths? God hates sin; His presence will not enter an unkept dwelling place. He who takes time to commune with Him grows.

As Christians, our actions must shine as lights set on a hill (Zion), to the lost around us. As priests, we must stir our brothers and sisters in the Lord to righteous living. As previously stated, Christ made the provision; it's up to the individual to determine how closely he lives with Jesus.

VI

DANCE IN THE FEAST

"Blessed, happy, fortunate, to be envied, are the people who know the joyful sound, who understand and appreciate the spiritual blessing symbolized by the feast, they walk, Oh Lord, in the light and favor of thy countenance."

Psalms 89:15 (Amplified Bible)

Oh how God's people loved to celebrate their God! Let's have a gathering; let's parade before the whole world - let's make known His greatness! Natural Israel was a nation who knew how to celebrate their God. They were a dancing and singing nation. As Christians, we should be joyful in our God and let joy be our witness to an unhappy world. We must look at natural Israel and her feast days to glean the vision God wants us to see. Also we must look for our spiritual prophetic fulfillment in Christ.

"Think not that I am come to destroy the law, or the prophets: I am not come to destroy, but to FULFILL."

Matthew 5:17

We must experience the vision as believers. The feast days were holy days, days of gathering together to remember what God did for His people. Pay attention to that "joyful sound" we hear spreading like wind across the land. God's

people, spiritual Israel, that new nation, the Church, is RIS-
ING UP these days with JOY in their HEARTS and FEET.

There are seven major feast days that the Lord commanded Israel to celebrate throughout the generations. These
are found in *Leviticus 23 and Deuteronomy 16:*

> *"And the Lord spake unto Moses, saying, Speak unto
> the children of Israel, and say unto them, Concerning
> the feasts of the Lord, which ye shall proclaim to be
> holy convocations, even these are my feasts."*
>
> *Leviticus 23:1-2*

> *"These are the feasts of the Lord, even holy convoca-
> tions, which ye shall proclaim in their seasons."*
>
> *Leviticus 23:4*

> *". . . it shall be a statute for ever throughout your
> generations in all your dwellings."*
>
> *Leviticus 23:14, 21, 41*

These feasts are divided into three time periods we will
call "feast periods." All of these Old Testament feasts reveal
Christ; His plan, His purpose, His times and His seasons. The
feasts also show the calendar of "God's Timetable."

The Tabernacle - God's plan for building order and
structure.

The Feast - God's timetable, calendar of events.

PASSOVER

The feast of Passover was observed in three parts:
1.   Passover
2.   Unleavened bread
3.   First fruits

It ususally took place around March or April. The
fourteenth day of the first month was Passover. The fifteenth
day was the feast of unleavened bread. A few days later the

feast of first fruits was celebrated. This feast celebrated the great deliverance from Egyptian bondage under the hand of Moses. What this feast means to the Christian is three-fold:

1. We are to recognize and remember the great deliverance God wrought on behalf of His people as a nation.

2. We are to recognize Jesus Christ as our passover Lamb.

> *"The next day John seeth Jesus coming unto him, and saith, "Behold the Lamb of God, which taketh away the sin of the world."*
>
> *John 1:29*

> *"But with the precious blood of Christ, as of a lamb without blemish and without spot."*
>
> *I Peter 1:19*

3. Application to ourselves.

We can readily celebrate this feast in truth. Christ has freed us from the bondage of sin and protected us from destruction. It is a privilege to celebrate forever the work of passover.

This feast was to be remembered with GREAT gladness:

> *"And the children of Israel that were present at Jerusalem kept the feast of unleavened bread seven days with great gladness: and the Levites and priests praised the Lord day by day, singing with loud instruments unto the Lord."*
>
> *II Chronicles 30:21*

> *"And kept the feast of unleavened bread seven days with joy: for the Lord had made them joyful. . ."*
>
> *Ezra 6:22*

Every able-bodied male of each family was commanded by God to come to Him to celebrate the feast. The people made a pilgrimage to Jerusalem's temple to observe the feast. Many had to camp along the walls of the city because there were so many people prepared to celebrate. Many had traveled in joyous processions led by flutes and pipes. Small timbrels played by the women helped to keep all in step with the march to the feast.

> *"Ye shall have a song, as in the night when a holy solemnity is kept; and gladness of heart, as when one goeth with a pipe to come into the mountain of the Lord, to the mighty One of Israel."*
>
> *Isaiah 30:29*

Once at the temple site, the people with their sacrifices could hear the Levites accompanying the singers or choir with all their instruments. The Priests stood in rows to receive the lamb which was killed by the owner himself. There would be song and dance and music from the platform of the Levitical ministers, day by day and hour by hour.

The next aspect is the feast of unleavened bread. Paul says in *I Corinthians:*

> *"Therefore let us keep the feast, not with old leaven, neither with the leaven of malice and wickedness; but with the unleavened bread of sincerity and truth."*
>
> *I Corinthians 5:8*

Each home was to be swept clean. All manner of leaven destroyed. Leaven refers to sin, and we as Christians are to put away all manner of sin and unrighteousness. Sin is our fault and this can only be washed away with the blood of the Lamb. A root problem can never be washed away but by the power of the cross of Jesus Christ. *Romans 6:1-10* says that sin can only be destroyed by the continual working of the cross. This feast commanded the children of Israel to eat unleavened bread for seven days. This typifies the continual eating of the Word of God, the continual application of the cross to our hearts. The feast of unleavened bread is symbolized by the sanctification done in our lives. Positional sanctification was granted to us by the Passover Lamb and practical sanctification is wrought in us as we walk. One who continues to be liberated from sin will respond with joy flowing from experience to experience. Praise the Lord! Let's dance!

The final aspect is the feast of First Fruits. This brings in our first offerings unto the Lord - first fruits in harvest, work of our hands - Christ is the First Fruit of the resurrection.

> *"But now is Christ risen from the dead, and become the first fruits of them that slept. For since by man came death, by man came also the resurrection of the dead. For as in Adam all die, even so in Christ shall all be made alive."*
>
> *I Corinthians 15:20-22*

The first sheaf of the barley harvest was gleaned and offered as first fruits with great joy and celebration in the fields. This feast is both joyful and solemn. It was officially entitled the season of liberation or season of joy.

Two distinct times in Israel's history she wandered from celebrating Passover. She became entangled in the idol worship surrounding her. This principle holds true today. Let's dance, sing, act, paint, unto Jesus! Beware of using your talent for other gods. Under King Hezekiah of Judea and King Josiah of Judah, the feast of Passover was reinstated. They were bringing the people back to the celebrations of the Lord.

Our record of Jesus celebrating the Passover is in *Matthew 26:17, Luke 22:15 and I Corinthians 5:7-8*. After the destruction of the temple in 70 A.D. by the Romans, the Passover continued to be celebrated in homes and local synagogues. After celebrating the Passover meal, all would rise to sing praises unto God. The Hallel was always sung *(Psalms 113-118)*. The main dance of Passover is the procession. Part of the Passover meal called the Sedar continued down through history to be used for the Sabbath. Many today do a dance called "Greeting of the Sabbath." The holy day was always greeted with song and dance.

PENTECOST

The second feast period is the Feast of Weeks or Pentecost. This feast began fifty days after First Fruits and the name Pentecost means "fifty." It was fifty days after Israel was set free from the Egyptian bondage that God visited them on Mt. Sinai. Another name for this feast is Feast of Harvest. This feast always occurred early in the summer. This was the second time of the year all able-bodied Jewish men were commanded by God to appear before Him. At the Temple in Jerusalem, many, many devout Israelites were joyfully waiting to respond to God. For this feast, the people were to bring two wave loaves made of newly harvested wheat and flour. This feast was also known as a festival of thanksgiving. The people rejoiced in the fruit of the land. It was also considered the season of the giving of the Law. The past aspect of this feast is considered to be the birthday of Judism because of the Law given at Mt. Sinai on Pentecost. To the Christian it signifies the birth of the church as seen in *Acts 2:1-5*. The old covenant was fulfilled by a new and better covenant:

> *"And when the day of Pentecost was fully come, they were all with one accord in one place."*
>
> *Acts 2:1*

For us this feast signifies the gift of the Holy Spirit. We know that leaven is symbolic of sin, and this is the only time that cereal offerings were made with leaven. At Pentecost the church is made up of Jew and Gentile alike. Now we see why two loaves were offered - for the church of both Jew and Gentile WITH SIN. The Passover represented Christ, the unleavened bread WITHOUT SIN. Those 3,000 Jews and Gentiles were the first fruits of the church.

The book of *Ruth* celebrates the joining of Gentile and Jew. Ruth, a Gentile woman came to know and love the God of Naomi, a Jewish woman. *Matthew 1:5-16* acknowledges Jesse's seed, from Ruth and Boaz which begat Jesus Christ.

The main dances of this feast were the procession and the round or circle dance.

> *"Seven weeks shalt thou number unto thee: begin to number the seven weeks from such time as thou beginnest to put the sickle to the corn. And thou shalt rejoice before the Lord thy God, thou, and thy son, and thy daughter, and thy manservant, and thy maidservant, and the Levite that is within thy gates, and the stranger, and the fatherless, and the widow, that are among you, in the place which the Lord thy God hath chosen to place his name there."*
>
> *Deuteronomy 16:9, 11*

The people rejoiced while gathering the harvest and giving the offering to the Lord. An example of a Jerusalem procession for Pentecost would be one of singing men and women. Women and children dancing and playing happily as they worshipped their God. Flower garlands were woven for the young girls' hair. Men marched to the music being piped as they moved closer to their appointed place of offering.

FEAST OF TABERNACLES

The third great feast period is called the Feast of Tabernacles. This great feast brought the promise of the land to the people of Israel. Another word for Feast of Tabernacles is "Chag Adony," meaning "God's festival." Chag is the root word for religious dance, the procession of the festival.

> *"And thou shalt observe the feast of tabernacles seven days, after that thou hast gathered in thy corn and wine: And thou shalt rejoice in thy feast, thou, and thy son, and thy daughter, and the manservant, and thy maidservant, and the Levite, the stranger, and the*

fatherless, and the widow, that are within thy gates. Seven days shalt thou keep a solemn feast unto the Lord thy God in the place which the Lord shall choose: because the Lord thy God shall bless thee in all thine increase, and in all the works of thine hands, therefore thou shalt surely rejoice. Three times in a year shall all thy males appear before the Lord thy God in the place which he shall choose; in the feast of unleavened bread, and in the feast of weeks, and in the feast of tabernacles: and they shall not appear before the Lord empty."

Deuteronomy 16:13-16

The word feast in these passages of scripture is "chagag" meaning: a feast, a dance. In *Exodus 23:14-16* the word "feast," or in Hebrew "chagag," is interpreted as a procession. In *Exodus 34:22* the word "feast," or "chagag" is interpreted to mean "circle or procession."

This feast is one in which the men became involved in the dancing and the worship. There was always a procession to the altar and a circle dance around the altar. According to some opinions, it was during tabernacles that the daughters of Shiloh danced in the vineyards in *Judges 21:21*. Other references to this feast before the temple was built are found in *I Kings 8:2; I Samuel 1*. Here the people marched joyously in sacred procession singing hymns and playing instruments.

Amos and Hosea protested the way the people of Israel overemphasized drinking and eating. The real purpose of the feast had been overlooked *(Amos 5:21-27, Hosea 9:1, Isaiah 28:7-8, Exodus 32:5)*.

True praise and worship is restored after Baal is defeated, and the festivals were brought into the temple to be supervised. The Feast of Tabernacles has three main parts: Trumpets, Day of Atonement, and Tabernacles. The first part, Trumpets, had not been heard over the city of Juerusalem or Israel as an atonomous state since 586 B.C. However, in 1967, Israel became a nation and the Shofar was heard, which signifies a new awakening for the people. *Numbers Chapter Ten,* lists the nine works of the trumpets:

1)   The first signal was for calling an assembly. When we hear this sound coming forth we are to think of unity in the church. This trumpet has been sounding forth for a while. *Psalms 133* tells us how powerful and beautiful the unity of the brethren is, for it's there God commands His blessing "Life."

2)   The second trumpet signal was for journeyings. When God is ready to move, He lets us know through His trumpets, the prophetic voice of the Lord. We are challenged to rise up and move on in God when this trumpet sounds.

3)   The third signal of trumpets is for gathering of the princes. Princes signify leadership. *"The heads of the thousands shall gather unto me"* in *verse four* represents a new unity in Jesus; the ministry coming together.

4)   The fourth signal of trumpets is for sounding an alarm. It's as if God blows the whistle against heresy, false doctrine and false teachers. Trumpets sounding while preparing for war against the enemy of the church "humanism."

5)   Going to war is acknowledged by the fifth signal of the trumpets. Let's rise up now and possess areas for God. When we hear this sound, we can rise up and take the offensive for Jesus. We can march ahead knowing He will go before us because we heard His "trumpet."

6)   The sixth trumpet blast signals a day of gladness. It is time to worship and rejoice; to celebrate our God. This joyful sound releases us to take time to enjoy God.

7)   The seventh signal of the trumpet heralds solemnity. This is the sound of prayer and fasting. With reverence and fear we humbly bow before our God in prayer.

8)   The eighth is for the beginning. God always lets us know when we turn a corner and begin a new day in Him.

9)   The last signal listed in *Chapter Ten of Numbers* is the trumpets sounding over the sacrifices. Our sacrifices and offerings are given with a heart of worship, full of song unto the Lord.

The second phase of Tabernacles is the Day of Atonement. This feast began ten days after trumpets. There is a dance associated with this feast. It is a mourning circle dance and a procession. When a fast was called by the High Priest, this procession was done with wailing up to the temple mount. Then a prayer was offered up for the forgiveness of sins. These ten days of repentance will grant unto the people either life or destruction, riches or poverty, health or sickness. This is the time to be reconciled to God. This service began at sundown with psalms of forgiveness sung by three individuals. All three were dressed in white. They lead the people in "all vows," a prayer asking forgiveness for lack of keeping vows. At the temple, the High Priest, assisted by 500 other priests and Levites fasted and prayed while one High Priest entered beyond the veil with the atoning blood. As the priest came out of that Holy of Holies, the people sighed with relief, for their sins were forgiven for another year.

> *"But Christ being come an high priest of good things to come, by a greater and more perfect tabernacle, not made with hands, that is to say, not of this building; neither by the blood of goats and calves, but by his own blood he entered in once into the holy place having obtained eternal redemption for us."*
>
> *Hebrews 9:11-12*

Possessing remission of sins by Jesus Christ according to Hebrews gives us boldness to enter into the holiest of holies.

After the Day of Atonement came the most festive celebration of all, the Feast of Tabernacles. This feast is a time of ingathering, a time of great joy. All the people were commanded to build booths and dwell in them seven days to remember dwelling in tents during their wandering in the wilderness. This was a time to bring free will offerings and tithes unto God. This feast occurs around the end of September or early October.

> *"Also in the fifteenth day of the seventh month, when ye have gathered in the fruit of the land, ye shall keep a feast unto the Lord seven days: on the first day shall*

*be a sabbath, and on the eighth day shall be a sabbath.
And ye shall take you on the first day the boughs of
goodly trees, branches of palm trees, and the boughs of
thick trees, and willows of the brook; and ye shall
rejoice before the Lord your God, seven days. And ye
shall keep it a feast unto the Lord seven days in the
year. It shall be a statute for ever in your generations;
Ye shall celebrate it in the seventh month. Ye shall
dwell in booths seven days, all that are Israelites born
shall dwell in booths: That your generations may know
that I made the children of Israel to dwell in booths,
when I brought them out of the land of Egypt: I am the
Lord your God."*

Leviticus 23:39-43

It is significant of the harvest of God's abundance. The
harvest is brought in from the orchards, fields and groves.
Another name for this feast is the feast of ingathering, truly a
thanksgiving feast. Celebrations of this feast were full of singing and dancing.

The first section of this feast is called "the drawing out
of the water." A libation is poured out upon the altar. As a
sign of prayers for abundant rain, the latter rain, Israel could
expect a full harvest. This could be called a visual demonstration of what God's grace could do in granting an abundance
of rain. While the priest poured out the water, the choir sang
the Hallel. There was a beautiful procession from the temple
down to the Spring of Shiloam and back again. A pitcher of
wine was also poured out to mix with the water. Levites with
their trumpets trumpeted. The procession moved. The people
waved their palm branches. There were such crowds in town
that every Levite had to be on duty. During the course of the
singing, the procession moved toward the altar. The worshippers danced in procession around the altar. This was done
once every day for seven days. The seventh day was called the
Day of Great Hosannah. Jesus spoke also of the great feast
day. His quote in *John 7:37-39* was spoken on this great
day.

"In the last day, that great day of the feast, Jesus stood and cried, saying, If any man thirst, let him come unto me, and drink. He that believeth on me, as the scripture hath said, out of his belly shall flow rivers of living water. (But this spake he of the Spirit, which they that believe on Him should receive: for the Holy Ghost was not yet given; because that Jesus was not yet glorified)."

What an outpouring we have through the Holy Spirit!

"But this is that which was spoken by the prophet Joel: And it shall come to pass in the last days, saith God, I will pour out of my Spirit upon all flesh: and your sons and your daughters shall prophesy, and your young men shall see visions, and your old men shall dream dreams: and on my servants and on my handmaidens I will pour out in those days of my spirit; and they shall prophesy."

Acts 2:16-18

The last part of this great feast is called the Feast of Illumination. Another name for this is the Torch Dance. It was done at night to light the candles on the lamps. The dance begins in the court of the women. Four golden candleabras were filled with oil. Men would dance before the people with flaming torches as they sang psalms and praise songs. The Levites with their harps, lutes, cymbals, and trumpets played hymns while all sang with their voices resounding the praises of God. These dances began on the 15th step and traveled up and down according to the "15 Song of Degrees" in *Psalms.* Many sang the Songs of Ascents in *Psalms 120-134.* As the morning rooster crows, the Levites sound the trumpet and the celebration is done *(John 8:12, Matthew 5:14-16).* Today the ninth day of Tabernacles is called Simchas Torah or "rejoicing in the law." Here men and women promenade in the synagogue carrying scrolls of the Word of God. One singer leads the procession of marching, singing people. Flags and banners waving, bells ringing; seven times the dance circles the platform. Children bearing flags and candles march in order. This is a joyous procession done colorfully and expressively. The flags are of the tribe of Judah. Judah means Praise. Let us praise God in joyous procession!

The feast of Dedication is listed only once in the New Testament.

> *"And it was at Jerusalem the feast of the dedication, and it was winter. And Jesus walked in the temple in Solomon's porch."*
>
> *John 10:22-23*

Also called Festival of Lights or Hanukkah, it began around 164 B.C. Syrian rule over Jerusalem had polluted the temple. A number of devout Jews resisted this offensive act and eventually drove the Syrians from the city. Judas Maccabees cleansed the temple and restored the order of worship. This cleansing of the temple took place on December 25 and the celebration continued for eight days. This feast is done with great rejoicing and singing. Palm branches were waved in procession as the people sang the Hallel. Beautiful lights glowed all over the city; Jesus is the light of the world. We are the temple not made with hands.

> *"Know ye not that ye are the temple of God, and that the Spirit of God dwelleth in you?"*
>
> *I Corinthians 3:16*

Christ is the temple cleanser and the temple illuminator. We can dedicate our bodies, souls, and spirits totally unto the Lord who lives and dwells in us.

The last feast I want to cover is the Feast of Purim. This feast was to commemorate the story of Esther. It is celebrated with dancing where the feet stamp the ground. It was a "feast of lots," showing a casting of lots for the destruction of Haman. Esther, a fair maiden, was chosen of God to be the vessel to save the nation of Israel. Though doom and destruction loomed brightly on every corner, God's divine providence brought victory, joy and gladness which replaced fasting and mourning.

> *"And Mordecai went out from the presence of the king in royal apparel of blue and white and with a great crown of gold, and with a garment of fine linen and purple; and the city of Shushan rejoiced and was glad. The Jews had light, and gladness, and joy, and honor. And in every province and in every city, whithersoever the king's commandment and his decree came, the Jews had joy and gladness, a feast and a good day. And many of the people of the land became Jews; for the fear of the Jews fell upon them."*
>
> *Esther 8:15-17*

God can bring deliverance from the oppressor to His people. With each victory comes a church that celebrates the spiritual feast of Purim. As we participate in all these feasts, I am confident to stand with God's Word that many people will SEE and be saved. Be confident also that a church that dances will not bring a reproach!

VII

A WELLSPRING OF JOY

The Bible has much to say about joy. The word "joy" in the dictionary means:

1) An emotion of keen or lively pleasure, arising from present or expected good.

2) A source or cause of gladness and delight.

Your joy can either be your SOURCE of gladness or your CAUSE of gladness. When one accepts Jesus as their personal Savior, He graciously deposits deep within every believer a well - salvation. What does a well do? It is the source of or container for water. Our life-giving water is the Holy Spirit.

Most people relate joy to happiness, but they are two very different things. Happiness depends upon circumstances; joy comes from deep within and is not dependent upon our environment. Upon salvation, our "well" sustains us.

> "For the kingdom of God is not meat and drink; but righteousness, and peace and joy in the Holy Ghost."
> Romans 14:17

It is the joy of the Lord that transforms us. It turns our energy into life. It gives us strength for every day.

> "Then he said unto them, Go your way, eat the fat, and drink the sweet, and send portions unto them for whom nothing is prepared: for this day is holy unto

your Lord; neither be ye sorry; for the joy of the Lord
is your strength."

Nehemiah 8:10

These days are days of darkness, and it is going to be the
joy of the Lord that causes the world to notice. A people that
enjoy God's presence will be a dancing, singing people. Circumstances and life experiences only help to enlarge the capa-
city for joy.

"They that sow in tears shall reap in joy."

Psalms 126:5

Our joy depends upon the reservoir within, and not the
circumstances without.

WORLD	KINGDOM
Be hungry	Eat
Be thirsty	Drink
Be ashamed	Rejoice
Cry for sorrow	Sing for joy
Howl for vexation of spirit	*Isaiah 65:13-14*

The Christian should live in perpetual joy. It is our way
of life. It flows from within us eternally.

The world is now looking to the church and her joy.
Outside of Christ, life is gloom, despair, frustration, criticism
and darkness.

Where is your water level? You must draw from the
waters of life with your bucket - the bucket called joy!

"Therefore with joy shall ye draw water out of the
wells of salvation."

Isaiah 12:3

We all have our "bad days." By drawing with joy (our
bucket) we can draw all the strength we need. *II Corinthians*

6:10.

> *"As sorrowful, yet always rejoicing. . ."*

> *"Rejoice evermore." I Thessalonians 5:16.*

We sing a chorus that says:

> "Joy is the flag that is flown from the castle of my heart that the King is in residence there."

Amen! Let's rise up as believers and fly that flag of joy so the nations will see the King is in residence. Joy flowing like a river will illumine the handiwork of God. Rivers of living water will flow to dry and thirsty nations. The prophets spoke about it in *Isaiah 32:13 & 15.*

> *"Upon the land of my people shall come up thorns and briers; Yea upon all the houses of joy in the joyous city. . . Until the spirit be poured upon us from on high. . . "*

> *"Sing, O heavens; and be joyful, O earth; and break forth into singing, O mountains: for the Lord hath comforted his people, and will have mercy upon his afflicted."*
>
> *Isaiah 49:13*

That day is come; people are steeped in depression and have no hope.

> *"And it shall come to pass in that day, that the mountains shall drop down new wine, and the hills shall flow with milk, and all the rivers of Judah shall flow with waters, and a fountain shall come forth of the house of the Lord, and shall water the valley of Shittim."*
>
> *Joel 3:18*

Jesus met the woman at the well and instructed her concerning the issues of life.

> ". . . but the water that I shall give him shall be in him a well of water springing up into everlasting life."
> John 4:14

This woman chose to receive the water of life. We can choose to enter in with joy or work at being discouraged. The church must activate the wellspring and let waters of life and rivers of joy flow out. This is why we dance!

YET I WILL REJOICE IN THE LORD, I

WILL JOY IN THE GOD OF MY SALVATION.

VIII

A DANCE COMPANY

The word "dance" in some places of scripture has a slightly different meaning then what we have covered. In most places, the Hebrew word describes what type of dance is being done, but in a few places it describes who is dancing. The Hebrew word of dance in some scripture is "Macholah." This translation is a dance company; a troop, sometimes with chorus. It is a noun, while "machol" also a noun, is a round dance; a company of dancers.

A.   *Exodus 15:20*

"And Miriam the prophetess, the sister of Aaron, took a timbrel in her hand; and all the women went out after her with timbrels and with DANCES.*"

*Macholah - a dance company, troop, dances.

B.   *Judges 21:21*

"And see, and, behold, if the daughters of Shiloh come out to DANCE* in DANCES,** then come ye out of the vineyards, and catch you every man his wife of the daughters of Shiloh, and go to the land of Benjamin."

*Chul-chil - to twist or whirl in a circular or spiral man-

ner.
**macholah - a dance company, dances.

C.   *Song of Solomon 6:13*

      "Return, return, O Shulamite; return, return,
      that we may look upon thee. What will ye see in
      the Shulamite? As it were the COMPANY* of
      two armies."

*Macholah - dance company. Also translated a singing
company of dancers.

D.   *Psalms 68:25*

      "The singers went before, the players on instru-
      ments followed after; among them were the
      damsels PLAYING* with timbrels."

*sachaq - to rejoice, make merry, laugh in pleasure, to
play.

E.   *I Samuel 18:6; I Samuel 21:11*

      "And it came to pass as they came, when David
      was returned from the slaughter of the Philistine,
      that the women came out of all cities of Israel,
      singing and DANCING,* to meet king Saul, with
      tabrets, with joy, and with instruments of music."
*macholah - a dance company, dances.

F.   *I Samuel 29:5*

      "Is not this David, of whom they sang one to
      another in DANCES,* saying, Saul slew his thous-
      ands, and David his ten thousands?"
*macholah - dance company, dances.

G.   *Jeremiah 31:4*

> *"Again, I will build thee, and thou shalt be built, O virgin of Israel: thou shalt again be adorned with thy tabrets, and shall go forth in the DANCES* of them that make merry."*

*macholah - dance company, dances.

From these references, we can see a company of dancers that set forth to lead the people in dances. David's Tabernacle is a pattern of divine appointment.

> *"And David spake to the chief of the Levites to appoint their brethren to be the singers with instruments of music, psalteries and harps and cymbals, sounding, by lifting up the voice with joy. . ."*
>
> *I Chronicles 15:16-22*

Leadership has the ability and the authority to appoint a dance company that would minister unto the Lord. It is also vital that they set in order duties of that company as well as the leader of the group. Normally someone who is faithful, a servant, and most of all, a worshipper is chosen. If someone can't lift their hands in worship, how can they dance?

A dance company will function much the same as an appointed choir or orchestra. They need practice time in preparation for their ministry. As one becomes more involved in this ministry, natural as well as spiritual readiness is vital. They must have the ability to spontaneously dance with joy at the request of the worship leader as well as prepare special dances. The more involved one becomes, the more dedication and preparation is required. . . dedication to pre-service prayer; dressing appropriately for dance at every service; being able to respond to leadership, etc.

The Dance Company is a group of people set apart to minister in this area. Why have a company of dancers or a choir? They are to lead forth the people:

WHY WE DANCE

COMPANY	CONGREGATION
We dance to create or CAUSE an atmosphere for God's Presence	We dance because of the EFFECT of God's Presence

COMPANY	CONGREGATION
To wait, bear - Chul chil (Heb)	Joyful - Gul Gil (Heb)
Bring forth - Chul chil (Heb)	Whirl - Karar (Heb)
Drive away - Pazaz (Heb)	Twist - Chul Chil (Heb)
Stamp - Rekad (Heb)	Leap - Mallomai (Greek)
Shout - Choros (Greek)	Jump - Skirtao (Greek)
Grieve - Chul Chil (Heb)	Skip - Rekad (Heb)
Writhe - Chul Chil (Heb)	Spring about - Rekad (Heb)
Travail - Chul Chil (Heb)	
Spin - Gul Gil (Heb)	

A different responsibility is placed on those in the company and those who are not. It is the same as the choir or orchestra. The dance company is responsible for leading out with the right dance. This prevents the congregation from doing their own thing. When the service is joyous and the Holy Spirit tells His people to respond, the dance company has anticipated this. The company moves ahead to its position in order to lead the people. The divine scriptural order says the company goes out first and leads the congregation in joy and triumph. Sometimes the congregation will join in and other times the congregation will praise God through the ministry of the dancers. The congregation can be lifted as one by following leadership into the dance experience.

Another purpose of a company of dancers is simply to praise the Lord! A dancer's body is an instrument yielded to the power of the Holy Spirit. The singers use voices, the orchestra use instruments, and the dancers use their bodies. This should not in any way bring a reproach to the Name of the Lord; but represent grace, beauty and purity. The dance becomes a channel for God's power and blessing. By ministering unto the Lord first, the dancer releases blessings to the people.

Sometimes simple hand movements of praise can lead a whole people into His presence by group participation. Other times, the dancers would be moved upon by the Holy Spirit to dance purely on the King's command. This is a communion between the dancer and her Lord Jesus. He alone becomes the partner.

A dance ministry brings liberation to a people. A dancer must not only be liberated in herself but have the ability to liberate others. A company responding to the stirring power of the Holy Spirit can cause the people to rise up out of complacency to move with God.

> *"And it shall come to pass, as soon as the soles of the feet of the priests that bear the ark of the Lord, the Lord of all the earth, shall rest in the waters of Jordan, that the waters of Jordan shall be cut off from the waters that come down from above; and they shall stand upon an heap."*
>
> *Joshua 3:13*

> *"And the God of peace shall bruise Satan under your feet shortly. . ."*
>
> *Romans 16:20*

> *". . .Come near, put your feet upon the necks of these kings. And they came near, and put their feet upon the necks of them. And Joshua said unto them, fear not, nor be dismayed, be strong and of good courage: for thus shall the Lord do to all your enemies against whom ye fight."*
>
> *Joshua 10:24-25*

As the dance company moves out and dances a dance of deliverance, bondages and habits will be broken. It is not the dance alone, but the anointing of God that breaks every yoke, whether by song, dance or prophetic word. Dancers and singers were appointed by Jehosaphat to lead the people into battle.

> *"And when he had consulted with the people, he*

appointed singers unto the Lord, and that should praise
the beauty of holiness, as they went out before the
army, and to say, Praise the Lord; for his mercy endur-
eth for ever."

II Chronicles 20:21

The ones who take part in this ministry must be liberated worshippers. The dancers must be vessels that can bring the
presence of the Lord into a service. A vessel that is yielded
unto the Holy Spirit can become a channel for His power and
blessing to flow through.

There may be times when the people do not seem to be
lifting or moving ahead as they should and something must be
done in order to lift that hindrance. A channel needs to be
opened. When this has happened with us, the worship leader
will call for the dancers to minister before the Lord. The
people will stir and the anointing will come because of the
unity of praise. The blockage will be lifted.

It is the responsibility of each company member to
know what type of dance should be done when. It is also a
blessing to learn what instruments accompanied the different
types of dance. We know the tambourine is a symbol of
joy and gaity, as well as an instrument of warfare. It is important for the dancer and orchestra to know the sounds of the
instruments and when they should minister.

A dance company does not have to minister at every
service, yet they should be ready. They can be used as an evan-
gelistic outreach and in dramas and pageants. There is no
limit to the use of a company in the church. This is a group
that recognizes the sound of the Holy Spirit, and stands ready
to minister effectively.

IX

SCRIPTURAL REFERENCES

God is restoring joy to the Church. His mercy and grace has so overwhelmed us at times our only response is to leap and sing for joy.

"The Lord hath appeared of old unto me, saying, Yea, I have loved thee with an everlasting love: therefore with loving-kindness have I drawn thee. Again I will build thee, and thou shalt be built, O virgin of Israel: thou shalt again be adorned with thy tabrets, and shalt go forth in the dances of them that make merry."
Jeremiah 31:3-4

When the presence and power of the Holy Spirit begins to move upon a congregation, the worshippers will want to respond to the direction. Sometimes dance will come forth. It was an experience of the Old and New Testament believers.

TABLE OF DANCES

1) THE PROCESSION - A dance done in a processional-like order. A row or rank-like motion. Sometimes done with a harp or stringed instrument, to and around the altar. *Psalms 48:12, 42:4, 26:2.* Kinnor or Kithara-walking ministrel with his instrument. The idea was to process to the

altar, then revolve or move around it in a circular manner.

2)   MOURNING PROCESSION - A procession done with one flutist and two that lamented. *Jeremiah 9:20, Luke 7:32*. Lament in Hebrew means to beat, sing in a chant, wailing or moaning. *Amos 5:16, II Chronicles 35:25*. This was also a dance of fasting and solemn assembly. Hired mourners were present for the burial of King Josiah. *II Chronicles 35:25*. Solomon speaks about them in *Ecclesiastes 7:5, Amos 5:16, Matthew 9:23, Mark 5:38*. A company of women were hired for this purpose; to dance and sing about the one who died. A tambourine and clapping kept the skilled dancers going.

3)   DANCE OF DELIVERANCE - As the song of deliverance came forth, the feet were put to use along with clapping, *Psalms 32:7*. A song of deliverance, a shout, dance of deliverance, a stamp or shake. The sound of deliverance is also heard in the flute, harp and cymbals. *I Chronicles 15:16, Isaiah 13:2, II Samuel 22:40-45, Isaiah 26:6, Psalms 29:6, 114:6*.

4)   THE ASCENT PROCESSION OR "ENTRANCE" - *Psalms 120 - 134* are called the songs of degrees. The dance done in *Psalms 68:25*. A rank or row like dance. *I Chronicles 26:16, II Chronicles 9:4*. Often done to flute. *Isaiah 30:29*. The entrances or ascent processional is a call to worship. Done on way up temple mount. David danced to bring up the ark. *I Chronicles 15:29, II Samuel 6:21*.

5)   THE WEDDING PROCESSIONAL - This dance was done in processional order to the groom's house by the bride and her maidens. Later in the ceremony a traditional circle dance was done around the bride and groom. *Song of Solomon 3:11, Isaiah 61:10, Genesis 29:33, 24:61;* Circle dance, *Psalms 30:11*.

6)   FEAST DANCE - Accompanied by harps and tambourines, this dance was done in a circle. *Psalms 118, Exodus 32:19* (negative).

7)   DANCE OF DEDICATION - A round dance done at the dedication of the temple. A circle or round dance in *Jeremiah 31:4, 13. Psalms 30:11*, a round dance. *Nehemiah 12:27*, a processional.

8)   DANCE OF GREETING - Usually done by women. Very close to a dance of victory, yet this was done to greet the Sabbath also. *Judges 11:34.*

9)   DANCE OF VICTORY - *Exodus 15:20,* dance done usually by a company with chorus and repeats. Great rejoicing. There were many palm branches waved by the people during a dance of victory. A circle or round dance or a joyous procession. *I Samuel 18:6, I Chronicles 15:29.*

10)   DANCE OF PRAISE AND WORSHIP - A round dance with chorus. Sometimes danced as a solo. *Psalms 149:3, 150:4, I Chronicles 16:30* (fear), *Psalms 96:9, 30:11.*

11)   DANCE OF ANNOINTING - Used with the flute to bring the presence of the Lord. *I Samuel 10:5-10, I Kings 1:40.*

12)   MEN'S DANCES - David is our example. *Isaiah 9:3, 61:10.* Usually at harvest, and great war experiences as well as feast days. *Jeremiah 31:13.*

This is just a very brief outline of the different types of themes in which dance was used. Every theme has a scriptural reference. According to Jewish history and traditions there are many more dances done to different *Psalms,* but we don't have scriptural references for them. In the original Hebrew, these dances are just a few that are accompanied with song:

1)   *Exodus 15:20* - Victory Dance (good)
2)   *Exodus 32:18-19* - Feast Dance (evil)
3)   *I Samuel 18:6, 7* - Victory Dance
4)   *I Samuel 21:11, 29:5* - Victory Dance
5)   *Psalms 26:6* - Altar Dance
6)   *Psalms 68:25* - Processional
7)   *Psalms 87:7* - Sanctuary

GOOD FOUNDATIONAL DANCE THEMES

A)   *Exodus 15:20* - A dance of rejoicing and great victory over the death of the enemy. Miriam led the company of women with the tambourine as they sang and danced before God. Also a dance of joy for entering into the promised land. We can dance for the future promise of what's ahead and for victory. The dance and joy will cause others to rise up in faith.

B)   *II Samuel 6:14-16* - The very presence of God was returning to its rightful place. We bring up the presence of God with dancing. Here King David took off his kingly robe, and dressed in a linen ephod as a priest to bless the Lord. He danced with all his might. God's presence is enough to cause anyone to dance.

C)   *Judges 21:21* - Every year to celebrate a great feast, the daughters of Shiloh came from every tribe to dance before the Lord. There were vineyards on the hillside where these young women danced.

D)   *Revelation 19:7* - *"Be glad and rejoice (leap for joy, turn about, spin) . . . for the marriage of the Lamb is come."* As we move closer to that appointed day, the Bride of Christ will dance even more.

E)   *Psalms 149:3, 150:4* - We are commanded by God's Word to praise Him in the dance. When we dance and rejoice before Him, He will bless!

F)   *I Samuel 18:6-7* - Here David and Saul come back from the battle. *"David has killed his ten thousands, Saul has killed his thousands."* This actually hadn't happened yet. Up to this point in time, David had only killed one bear, one lion and one Philistine. This shows the prophetic touch that rests in the dance. Dance was taught at the School of Prophets. It always brings the prophetic anointing.

There was a special place set apart for sacred dance. Some of our references take us into the sanctuary, while some are outside. The people danced at wells, village streets, vineyards, mountains, parks, threshing floors and fields. One such place of importance is called Ablemeholah - "The Meadow of the Dance." Here is where Gideon defeated his enemy. *(Judges 7:20-22)*. We can also defeat our enemies by putting them under our feet through the dance. Solomon's food came from this same place *(I Kings 4:7-12)*. Our strength is from the joy of the Lord. Elisha the prophet (with the double portion), was born in Ablemeholah *(I Kings 19:16)*. As we have said before, the prophetic anointing does rest on the dance.

HEBREW WORD STUDY

1)   CHUL; CHIL - to twist or whirl (in a circular or spiral manner) ie. specifically to dance, to turn around, to dance in a circle, also to writhe in pain, to bring forth, to travail. *Judges 21:21, 23* plus 13 more references.

2)   MACHOL - a round dance, dancing, chorus. *Psalms 30:11, 149:3, 150:4, Jeremiah 31:4, 13, Lamentations 5:15.*

3)   GUL; GIL - (Gool, Geel), to spin round (under the influence of any violent emotion) i.e. usually rejoice, or (as cringing) fear: be glad, joy, to go in a circle. *Psalms 2:11, 9:14, 13:4,5, 16:9, 21:1, 31:7, 32:11, 35:9, Zechariah 9:9,* plus 35 more references.

4)   MACHOLAH - A dance company or chorus, dances (fem. of Machol). *Exodus 15:20, Judges 11:34, 21:21, I Samuel 18:6, 21:11, 29:5, Song of Solomon 6:13, Jeremiah 31:4.*

5)   KARAR - to dance (whirl); to go or move in a circle. *II Samuel 6:14* to exult, leap, run.

6)   REKAD - to stamp, to spring about (wildly or for joy), dance, jump, leap, skip. *Psalms 29:6, 114:6, I Chronicles 15:29, Isaiah 13:21, Joel 2:5, Nahum 3:2.*

7)   DALAG - to spring or leap. *II Samuel 22:30, Psalms 18:29, Isaiah 35:6, Zephaniah 1:9, Song of Solomon 2:8.*

8)   PAZAZ - to leap, to bound, to be light agile. *Genesis 49:24, II Samuel 6:16.* To refine with fire (as gold) to solidify as if separating the limbs from the body, nimbly.

9)   CHAGAG - to move in a circle, specifically to march in a sacred procession, to observe a festival, to celebrate, idea of leaping, dancing in sacred dance, to reel to and fro. *Exodus 5:1, Leviticus 23:41, Exodus 23:14, Deuteronomy 16:16, Psalms 42:4, I Samuel 30:16.*

10)   CABAB - to revolve, surround or border, to re-

volve around a sacred object. *Psalms 26:6, 48:12.*

11)   HILIYKAH - a walking, procession or march, a caravan or company. *Psalms 68:24, 25.*

12)   SHUWR - to sing, as strolling along, minstrel, to turn, travel, strolling along with song. *Exodus 15:1, Psalms 33:3, 137:3, Jeremiah 20:13, Psalms 100:2, Isaiah 54:1, I Chronicles 15:27.*

13)   YADA - to use the hands (hold out), to revere or worship with extended hands, graceful gestures, to show or point out. *I Chronicles 16:4, Ezra 3:10, 11, Psalms 50:23, 107:8.*

14)   HALAL - to make a show, to boast, to be clamorously foolish, to celebrate.

15)   TOWDAH - extension of the hands, specifically a choir of worshippers, sacrifice of praise, thanks. *Jeremiah 33:11.*

GREEK WORD STUDY

1)   ORCHEOMAI - from "orchos", to dance in rank or regular motion, a row or ring. To put in rapid motion, a line dance, artistic. *Luke 7:32, Mark 6:22, Matthew 11:17, 14:6.*

2)   AGALLIAO - to jump for joy, be exceedingly glad or joyful. Rejoice used over sixteen times and translated as exceeding joy or greatly rejoice. Original Greek is "very much leaping." *Luke 1:14, 44, 47, 10:21, Matthew 5:12, John 5:35, 8:56, Acts 2:26, 46, 16:34, I Peter 1:6, 8, 4:13, Hebrews 1:9, Jude 24, Revelation 19:7.*

3)   HALLOMAI - to spring forth, to leap up. *Acts 3:8, 14:10.*

4)   EXALLOMAI - to spring forth, to leap up. *Acts 3:8.*

5)   SKIRTAO - to jump, sympathetically, move, leap for joy. *Luke 1:41, 44, 6:23.*

6)   CHORUS - a ring or round dance, chorus, dancing (a company of dancers and singers). A circular dance. *Luke*

15:25, Acts 6:5. Prochorus = Pro - leader, first. Chorus = dancer - Prochorus, a deacon was set in by the laying on of hands of the Apostles to be leader of the dance.

As we examine each reference and there are many more, we can see what type of steps were done to the dances.

X

CONCLUSION

With days of restoration upon us, we can expect those who come to embrace this visitation to move for the Kingdom of God. Skill and artistry in the areas of music, dance, drama, and art will be restored to the church. As we believe and rise up in faith we can take dominion over these areas and bring them under the hand of the church. This is the generation which is created to praise the Lord. Is this you? Once these areas belonged to God. They were ruled by Satan for a season. Now they are restored to give glory and honor to Jesus.

David's Tabernacle held the promise for the church. David taught divine order, divine judgement and the divine presence of God. Let's use the key to unlock the revelation of the kingdom that the nations would see and fear. Let us be symbols to all who believe and rejoice in the Lord.

Skill is evident - not fanaticism. A structured school in the local church is our training ground. A seed bed for tender truth revealed. How else can dance and song have any purpose but to be birthed out of this environment? Joy sets His church apart from the world. We take time to enjoy His presence. Through song and dance, He takes over our whole being. Formalism or ritual will kill that life. It causes death to the bearer and death to the observer. Creativity and vision will perish in this environment. A body may be diverse in administration of the arts. Creativity, vision, and outreach will be produced. Structure does not have to be void of life - Jesus is life!

What is artistry? It is beauty in an object. It is the quality in expression that distinguishes the artist from a technical person. It makes the difference between life and death. A church that dances out of tradition and ritual has no artistry. One that dances out the expression of an inner experience produces life. Artistry is a quality that can't be learned. It must be birthed from within. Artistry comes from life. That life is in the blood of Jesus Christ!

Dance was considered to be one of the mysteries of Christ. Only those who partook in this joy would feel the inner release of God's presence. Only as the church dances in faith does God's presence come upon their dance. He who dances must be released to leap for joy, or march in rank and order led by the Captain of the Host. All physical movement requires a yielding of ones body. This is the mystery. Not why some can or can't, but why some will and some won't. Dance has a relationship to life, death, and healing. It assists the living in their relationship with Jesus just as a song does. Dance inspired by the Word of God has power! It will release your will to live in Jesus. Allow the anointing of the Holy Spirit to descend in life-giving expression. ALL UNTO HIM!